D1116612

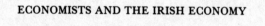

ECONOMISTS AND THE IRISH ECONOMY

ECONOMISTS AND THE IRISH ECONOMY
FROM THE EIGHTEENTH CENTURY
TO THE PRESENT DAY

edited by Antoin E. Murphy

IRISH ACADEMIC PRESS

in association with

HERMATHENA
TRINITY COLLEGE DUBLIN

330.9415
E19

This book was printed in the Republic of Ireland
for Irish Academic Press Limited, Kill Lane, Blackrock,
Co Dublin, and for *Hermathena,* Trinity College, Dublin.

It also appears as *Hermathena* CXXXV (Winter 1983).

ISBN 0 7165 2197 0

ISSN 0018 0750

© *Hermathena* 1984

Printed by Cahill Printers Ltd., East Wall Rd., Dublin 3.

Contents

ILLUSTRATIONS

University Libraries
Carnegie Mellon University
Pittsburgh, Pennsylvania 15213

Notes on Authors

LOUIS M. CULLEN
M.A. (N.U.I.), Ph.D. (Lond.), M.R.I.A. Professor of Modern Irish History, Trinity College, Dublin.

ANTOIN E. MURPHY
M.A. (N.U.I.), Barrister-at-Law. Senior Lecturer in Economics, Trinity College, Dublin.

CORMAC Ó GRÁDA
M.A. (N.U.I.), Ph.D. (Columbia). Statutory Lecturer in Economics, University College, Dublin.

TOM A. BOYLAN
B.A. (N.U.I.), M.Sc. (Dubl.). Statutory Lecturer in Economics, University College, Galway.

TADGH P. FOLEY
M.A., H.Dip.Ed. (N.U.I.), D.Phil. (Oxon.). Lecturer in English, University College, Galway.

ROBERT D. C. BLACK
M.A., B.Comm., Ph.D. (Dubl.), F.B.A., M.R.I.A., Honorary F.T.C.D. Professor of Economics, Queen's University, Belfast.

RONAN FANNING
B.A. (N.U.I.), Ph.D. (Cantab.). Statutory Lecturer in Modern Irish History, University College, Dublin.

SIR JOHN HICKS
F.B.A., Fellow of All Souls College, Oxford. Nobel Memorial Prize for Economics 1972.

NA

Foreword

by Antoin E. Murphy

In 1832 the chair of political economy was founded in Trinity College through the initiative and financial assistance of the Church of Ireland Archbishop of Dublin, Richard Whately. On the one hundred and fiftieth anniversary of this event it was felt appropriate to celebrate the establishment of this chair, one of the oldest in these islands, through a series of lectures on the theme *Economists and the Irish economy*. This volume reproduces the seven papers presented in this series. Additionally, an extra chapter on the circumstances surrounding the establishment of the chair of political economy in Trinity College is included.

The selection of the series title had a dual purpose. It was considered relevant (1) to indicate the contributions of some outstanding Irish economists to economic theory, and (2) to show the way in which economic phenomena in Ireland influenced economic theory, institutions and policy.

With reference to the first objective it is germane to point out that the output of Irish economists as an ethnic group has been little chronicled, to such an extent that J. K. Galbraith in his television series and book *The age of uncertainty* felt sufficiently emboldened to remark that 'All races have produced notable economists, with the exception of the Irish who doubtless can protest their devotion to the higher arts'. But Galbraith is not unique in this view for many Irish people, while prepared to tell visitors to this country of the glories of the Irish literary tradition and quoting Swift, Congreve, Goldsmith, Sheridan, Burke, Wilde, Shaw, Yeats, Joyce, Beckett, etc., at the same time know little of the contributions of Richard Cantillon, John Elliot Cairnes and Francis Ysidro Edgeworth.

Yet, these Irish economists are recognised as having made outstanding contributions to economics, Cantillon ranking alongside Francois Quesnay and Adam Smith as one of the great eighteenth-century economists, Cairnes being regarded in his day as 'second only to Mill himself' (J. N. Keynes, in *Dictionary of political economy*), while Edgeworth's *Mathematical psychics* has been described as 'probably the most elusively written book of importance in the history of economics' (G. J. Stigler, *Essays in the history of economics*).

Rather than concentrating exclusively on Trinity economists, holders of the Whately chair such as Longfield, Butt and Bastable,

9

or indeed discussing the contributions of Trinity educated contributors to economics such as George Berkeley, Francis Hutcheson, Edmund Burke, Robert Torrens, William Edward Hearn and John Kells Ingram, it was decided to analyse aspects of the career and work of the three most highly regarded Irish economists, Cantillon, Cairnes and Edgeworth. Thus Antoin Murphy contributed a paper on Richard Cantillon's banking career in Paris and his view on macroeconomic policy, which was contrasted with that of the Scotsman John Law. Tom Boylan and Tadgh Foley presented a paper on the way in which John Elliot Cairnes influenced John Stuart Mill's views on Ireland. Nobel prize winner in economics Sir John Hicks gave a paper on Francis Ysidro Edgeworth, one of his predecessors in the Drummond chair at Oxford and an economist 'who influenced much of my own early work on economic theory'. At the same time Professor R. D. C. Black, who has already made notable contributions on Mountifort Longfield, economic theory in Ireland in the nineteenth century, and the contributions of the Trinity School to value theory, presented a paper on 'The Irish dissenters and nineteenth century political economy' which reassessed the contribution of holders of the Whately chair such as Mountifort Longfield and Isaac Butt.

The second objective of the series was to have a number of papers dealing with the way in which economic phenomena in Ireland influenced economic theory, institutions and policy. Two years before the establishment of the Whately chair J. E. Bicheno made the following comment in *Ireland and its economy*:

I had long harboured the desire of visiting a country, which contradicts the received theory of population, and the established doctrines of political economists; where contrary to experience, the higher and lower orders profess different religions; and whence spring, as Pliny says of Africa in his time, all the marvellous and unaccountable contradictions of nature. Ireland is, therefore, to the moral and political philosopher what Australia is to the naturalist — a land of strange anomalies; and he must be a very dull observer, who does not bring home, from either of these countries, something new and interesting.

Banking, population developments, the great famine and the system of land tenure have provided economists with the anomalies referred to by Bicheno. Louis Cullen poses the problem as to why, after such a brilliant debut, Irish banking tended to stagnate in the second half of the eighteenth century. He shows the precocious growth of Irish banking and the way in which it was, unlike its

Foreword

Scottish counterpart, based almost exclusively on the activities of landlords. These landlord banks arose from the need of the landlord classes to transfer rents rather than from mercantile activity *per se*. After the 1750s the sharp rise in landlord rents made it possible for a rich gentry to dominate banking to such a degree that when their entrenched position was threatened by the growth of merchant banks they were instrumental in introducing an act in 1756 which for all practical purposes brought merchant banking to an end.

Cormac Ó Gráda raises the question as to whether Ireland was a case study in Malthusian economics. Surprisingly Malthus had little to say on pre-famine Ireland yet, to many, the Malthusian mould seemed a highly plausible one in which to examine the great famine. O'Grada is cautious about the application of the hard Malthusian orthodoxy to this appalling nineteenth-century tragedy.

While the contribution of Irish economists in the nineteenth century has been shown to be substantial, it is Ronan Fanning's belief that academic economists in Ireland offered little during the first thirty years of the newly established state. In a contentious paper Fanning maintains that the academic economists continued to cling to pre-Keynesian doctrines and that the catalyst for change came from the public service. In the non-Keynesian world of the 1980s the views of these academic economists may not seem as unfashionable as they were a decade ago.

ACKNOWLEDGEMENTS

The Department of Economics, Trinity College, wishes to thank the Provost of Trinity College, Dr W. A. Watts, the Vice-Provost, Professor Aidan Clarke, and the Dean of the Faculty of Economics and Social Studies, Professor John Bristow, for their assistance in launching this lecture series. A special word of thanks is due to Miss Nicola Lennon, the secretary of the Department, for the invaluable administrative services that she provided.

The Department is indebted to Professors Kieran Kennedy (E.S.R.I.), Peter Neary (U.C.D.), David O'Mahony (U.C.C.), Brendan Walsh (U.C.D.), two former holders of the Whately Chair, Professors George Duncan and Louden Ryan, and to the present holder of the chair, Professor Dermot McAleese, for chairing the sessions at which these papers were delivered.

11

Antoin E. Murphy

The Department also wishes to thank the editor of *Hermathena*, the Revd. J. R. Bartlett, for agreeing to devote a complete issue to this lecture series and for his editorial skills in preparing this volume.

Finally the Department wishes once again to express its gratitude to the contributors to this lecture series, particularly Sir John Hicks who delivered a memorable lecture on Francis Ysidro Edgeworth.

0322
Longfield, Mountifort 13-24

Mountifort Longfield's appointment to the chair of political economy in Trinity College, Dublin, 1832

by Antoin E. Murphy

On 31 October 1832 the first professor of political economy in Ireland was elected by the Board of Trinity College to assume the newly founded Whately professorship of political economy. The candidate chosen was Mountifort Longfield, a lawyer whose opening lectures, delivered in the Trinity and Michaelmas terms of 1833, entitle him to a prominent place in the history of nineteenth century economic thought.[1] In this, the one hundred and fiftieth anniversary of Longfield's accession to the Whately chair, it is relevant to trace some of the background developments to the establishment of one of the oldest chairs of economics in Britain and Ireland.

The background to Longfield's appointment gives a fascinating glimpse into the intervention of the founder of the chair, Archbishop Whately, in the University's selection process and the attitude of certain members of the Board on the criteria that they believed should be used in selecting a suitable candidate for the new chair.

This paper, using new sources of material — the Board Minutes and the diaries of two Board members, Dr Thomas Prior and Dr Franc Sadleir — shows the influence of Whately in the selection process and an important division of opinion within Trinity regarding the appointment of Longfield. It indicates that the suggestion that the Provost, Dr Bartholomew Lloyd, or indeed the Board, opposed the establishment of this chair is incorrect. The main issue that divided the Board seems to have been the political stance of the candidates for the chair. Through the investigation of this issue, a different view on Longfield's early political affiliations emerges than that attributed to him by historians of economic thought.

Richard Whately was appointed Church of Ireland Archbishop of Dublin in 1831. On accepting the archiepiscopal see of Dublin

*I am indebted to Professor R. D. C. Black (Queen's University, Belfast) and Professor R. B. D. McDowell (Trinity College, Dublin) for their most helpful suggestions and assistance in preparing this paper. The usual disclaimer applies.

13

Antoin E. Murphy

Whately resigned from his position as Drummond Professor of Political Economy at Oxford, in which he had succeeded his friend Nassau Senior, the first holder of the chair, in 1829. His comment on taking the chair at Oxford is of interest:

... some of my friends have persuaded me that this is a sort of crisis for the science in this place, such, that the occupying of the office by one of my profession and station may rescue it permanently from disrepute. Religious truth — which is, as you observe, the only description that calls for great sacrifices — appears to me intimately connected, at this time especially, with the subject in question. For it seems to me that before long political economists of some sort or other must govern the world; I mean that it will be with legislators as it is with physicians, lawyers, etc. — no one will be trusted who is not supposed at least to have systematically studied the sciences connected with his profession. Now the anti-Christians are striving hard to have this science to themselves, and to interweave with it their own notions . . .[2]

He was to say later, 'next to sound religion, sound Political Economy was the most essential to the well-being of society'.[3]

Despite the problems his church faced in Ireland at this time Whately regarded the establishment of a chair of economics, modelled on the Drummond chair, as a top priority. Richard Whately was consecrated Archbishop of Dublin on 23 October 1831. Returning to England to collect his family he arrived back in Dublin in mid-November. Within a matter of weeks he had opened up negotiations to found a chair of political economy. The Board minutes for 31 December 1831 state:

The Provost communicated the Archbishop of Dublin's proposal that a Professorship of Political Economy should be established in this University, he (the ArchB) endowing the same to the am^t of £100 p.An.[4]

The attitude of both the Board and the Provost to the Archbishop's proposal has so far been reported as hostile. W. J. Fitzpatrick in his *Memoirs of Richard Whately* suggested that 'If he (Whately) found a difficulty in popularizing the chair of Political Economy at Oxford, he found the difficulty increased tenfold in Dublin'.[5] He later reports Whately as saying many years later that 'they (the Fellows) thought that it was all a scheme of mine to blow up the University'.[6]

Yet if this was the case why did the Board make such a quick decision to allow the establishment of the new chair? Within three weeks of the Provost announcing the Archbishop's proposal to the Board a decision had been taken to establish the chair of political

14

Archbishop Richard Whately (by courtesy of the Representative Body of the Church of Ireland)

Antoin E. Murphy

economy. Furthermore Thomas Prior, who records the ensuing in-fighting on the selection of an appropriate candidate, does not mention any dissension at the Board on the principle of establishing this chair:

21 January 1832
Professorship of Polit[1] Economy funded by Arch Bishop of Dublin (Saly 100£ advertized open to graduates of Oxford, Cambridge and Dublin).[7]

From my reading of Prior's diary there is little doubt that this peppery and conservative senior fellow, seventy-five years old at the time, would have been only too happy to record any dissent, particularly as he had been greatly disappointed by his defeat in the previous year for the office of Provost. The role of the Provost, Bartholomew Lloyd, one of Trinity's great reforming Provosts, in the establishment of the chair has been misreported.[8] Moss has recently stated that 'Whately's suggestion that a chair of economics be established was at first opposed by the board and in particular, Provost Bartholomew Lloyd'.[9]

Moss bases this statement on Fitzpatrick's account of Whately's comments to the Dublin Statistical Society. However, it is obvious when comparing Fitzpatrick's account and the actual Report of the Address to the Dublin Statistical Society by Archbishop Whately that Fitzpatrick, and hence Moss, have misreported Whately.[10] It is quite clear that the Provost in communicating with Whately was passing on not his own personal view but that of certain members of the Board.

Rather than the Provost opposing Whately's proposal for the chair, it is evident from Dr Prior's account, published below, that he actively supported Whately. The areas of dissension that arose at the Board concerned the Archbishop's involvement in the selection of the professor of political economy and the criteria that should be used for judging the suitability of a candidate.

The Reverend Thomas Prior, Senior Lecturer in the College, 'quick to detect jobbery in arrangements for professorships', believed that the Archbishop improperly interfered from the outside in the academic selection process.[11]

In Prior's entry for May 1832 we find the first reference to this opposition:

Full Board. The Archbishop requested to examine and appoint Professor of Polit. Economy. Drs. Pr(ior), Ph(ipp)s, Hodg(kinson) against — carried 5:3!!!.[12]

16

Mountifort Longfield's appointment

The opponents of the Archbishop's appointment, Doctors Prior, Phipps and Hodgkinson, were all Tories.[13] Whately must have been informed of the opposition by some of the Senior Fellows to this procedure, as is evident from Prior's comments three days later on 22 May:

This day the Provost sent for me and read for me a letter from the Archbishop declining the honour of examining and appointing a Professor of Political Economy, but proposing to review essays written by the candidates so as to give his opinion and without knowing their names — it was a very long letter of 4 large pages protesting to have no object but the interest and honour of our university etc. I expressed my opinion against this scheme as compromising the authority and *dignity* of the Board. I proposed that he should call a Board, but he prefers endeavouring to obtain a majority of votes in this private manner and thus he succeeds sometimes in forestalling votes — a mode both troublesome to the members and injurious to the College.[14]

On Monday 9 July nine candidates, braving a bad outbreak of cholera in Dublin (the Board minutes mention a number of deaths from cholera), arrived at eleven o'clock in the morning to sit for the examination of the professorship of political economy. We know the names of four of these candidates: Haig, Hardy, Longfield and Newland. The examination lasted for two days with questions set by Whately, his friend Nassau Senior, and the registrar, Dr Robert Phipps. According to a Board minute for 9 July:

... a considerable number of questions in writing on the subjects connected with Pol. Econ. were given to each of them on which they wrote Essays in the Hall. These essays were afterwards perused by the Provost and Sen[r] Fellows.[15]

But behind the calm of this Board minute a major storm was brewing within Trinity. Dr Prior and Dr Phipps suspected that the selection of the professor of political economy was being stage-managed from the Archbishop's Palace with the active assistance of the Provost, Dr Lloyd. Prior, angered by what he believed was happening, wrote two long entries on the event as he viewed it in July:

12 July 1932
Election of Professor of Political Economy deferred until the pleasure of the Archbishop of Dublin, Dr. Whately, after having had nine candidates confined two days writing on subjects given by the Dr. Phipps and the

Antoin E. Murphy

Provost. The Provost forgetting the dignity of his station received (through Dr. Whately) questions from Mr. Senior, the Professor of Political Economy in Oxford, these questions he, on 9th July, gave to be written on by the candidates — on 10th July Dr. Phipps gave 4 subjects to be written on — the V. Provost declared he would vote on character — I could not possibly attend those candidates sooner than 13th July when I proposed to examine them, but the Provost thought it better to dismiss them on evening of 10th July unless I anxiously desired to examine on 12th — Of course I assented to their dismissal as he wishes, and they were so dismissed. They are naturally anxious to know — yet now on the 2nd day after their being dismissed, it is notified that Dr. Whately being absent in County of Wicklow no election can be held untill his return and opinion shall be known!!! — besides half the Board is now either absent or about being absent.

Dr. Whately and Lloyd are managing this most strangely. It had been communicated by the latter as the anxious wish of the former that the election should be made previous to long vacation for purpose of giving the Summer to the elected for preparing matter of his Winter lectures!!! — perhaps they have embryo Professor at present working.[16]

Whately read the answers of the candidates 'who were to reply under symbolical names; he being in perfect ignorance of the names of the candidates'.[17] Prior, in his entry of 28 July, did not believe this, suspecting that Dr Lloyd, the Provost, supplied the Archbishop with the names of the candidates. In this entry we find the first mention of Longfield, who appears as the front runner of the candidates:

28 July 1832
On the 28th inst, Doctor Wall deposited with me, essays and answers to written question, by 9 candidates for Professorship of Polit. Economy which essays and answers etc. had been left with him by Dr. Sadleir from Dr. Whately, Archbishop of Dublin, together with Dr. W———y's judgements and observations pointing out 3 of the candidates from whom selection ought to be made and also determining who of these would be the best Professor.

This day Dr. Sadleir called on me telling me he had a letter from the Provost saying that he had received a letter from Dr. W———y mentioning 3 any of whom might be elected — Dr. Sad^r stated also that the Provost agreed perfectly with W———y and wished the Board to elect without his (the Provost's) presence ———— the 3 selected are stated by Sad^r and Provost to be Longfield, Haig, Hardy and in this order of qualification ———— it is therefore in contemplation I suppose to make either Longfield or Haig the Professor, both of whom are radical politicians — Hardy would be a proper person, but his name is appended merely for some appearance of impartiality ————!!!

Mountifort Longfield's appointment

I immediately resolved not to read those papers which are so voluminous as to require at least 2 days for perusal. Dr. Wall informed me that they gave him a day and a half hard work ———————— I handed them over to Dr. Phipps who agreed with me that this proposed election is a farce and that there is no reason why I should have the trouble of inspecting those papers ———————— he agrees with me in thinking Doctor Newland would be the candidate most worthy of election from Character, the safest principle in which to elect in this case.

NB — the Archbishop affected to be ignorant of the candidates names, but his *congenial friend* the Provost (Dr. Lloyd) knew their names and he being mean enough to propose subjects and questions supplied *by the AB* (and one other) I doubt not in return supplied to him both the names and characters etc.[18]

Between July and October one of the three mentioned by Prior, Dr Haig, dropped out of contention to be replaced by the 'conservative' Dr Newland. The latter was strongly supported by the arch Tories on the Board, Doctors Prior and Phipps.

The Reverend Henry Newland, D.D., was vicar of Bannow, Co. Wexford, at this time. He was a conservative clergyman and a prolific writer.[19] The bulk of his writings were devoted to politico-religious issues in which he defended the interests of the established church. Despite applying for the chair of political economy he seems to have had little respect for the subject, disparagingly referring to the 'wildest spoliating political economist' in a work dealing with the tithes issue which was published in 1832.[20]

This was the type of man Prior and Phipps wanted in the chair, a person who favoured the *status quo* and was prepared to defend it actively. Newland seen in their light was an ideal candidate, a clergyman, a doctor of divinity and a man who had shown his mettle for political debate by crossing 'croziers' with the Catholic Archbishop of Dublin, Dr Doyle.[21]

But the voting of the Board on October 1832 favoured Mountifort Longfield rather than Dr Newland or even Mr Hardy.

31 October 1832
Professor of Political Economy elected — the Provost commenced by expressing a hope that the person elected should be one of 3 candidates recommended by ArchB Whately!!!

Drs. Hare, Wall, Sad^r voted for Dr. Longfield.
Drs. McD, Hodgk——————— for Mr. Hardy.

Antoin E. Murphy

Drs. Prior, Phipps ————— for Dr. Newland.
The Provost concurring with the majority Dr. Longfield was elected.[22]

It is interesting to attempt to disentangle the extent to which political affiliations rather than academic criteria were crucial in the selection process for the first holder of the chair. Prior and Dr Robert Phipps seemed to have decided that 'character', a euphemism for 'safe and sound conservatism', was the relevant criterion for this new position rather than the academic merit of the candidates. Prior, according to his own account, did not interview the candidates and refused to read the papers, deciding in a grossly unacademic manner that Newland was the most suitable candidate. Longfield was considered by Prior to be unsuitable as he was at the other end of the political spectrum — a 'radical politician' whose candidature was to be firmly opposed.

As Longfield has been characterised as being a political conservative when appointed to the chair, becoming a more liberal reformer towards the end of his life, it is worthwhile reading a little more into Prior's classification of him as a 'radical politician'.[23]

Prior was an extreme Tory but he was not alone amongst the Tories on the Board who opposed Longfield. He was supported by his ally, Dr Phipps, in supporting Newland, while another Tory, Dr Francis Hodgkinson, preferred Hardy. This trio, as has been shown, had already opposed Whately's involvement in the selection process, an opposition based on political rather than academic grounds.

Longfield, on the other hand, was supported by the Whig elements on the Board. The Provost had been appointed to office by the Whig government in 1831. Whilst not a 'committed Whig' it was at the same time hoped that 'he could be relied on to carry out a policy of reform consonant with which the new government was proposing in other fields'.[24] Prior's diary shows that the Provost worked very closely with Archbishop Whately on all issues relating to the new chair and was undoubtedly influenced by Whately, who was a Whig, as to who was the most suitable candidate.

Dr Franc Sadleir, the leading academic Whig at this time, seems to have been part of this group for he was the first to receive the papers after they had been read and judged by the Archbishop. Prior's words, 'the three selected are stated by Sad[r] and Provost to be Longfield, Haig and Hardy and in this order of qualification', suggest that Sadleir was also actively pushing the merits of Longfield.

20

Mountifort Longfield's appointment

It has not been possible to establish Dr Hare's political views but the other vote for Longfield was cast by Dr Wall who was known as a Tory. Wall, however, seems to have prided himself on being diligent and impartial in the academic process. His diligence is evidenced by the 'day and a half' of hard work that he spent on the papers. His impartiality and concern for the public interest comes through in the revulsion he expressed concerning an earlier incident involving Prior in nepotism in the Scholarship examination of 1825.[25]

Thus, while prepared to allow that Prior's categorisation of Longfield as a 'radical' may be somewhat extreme we are not prepared to accept the view that Longfield was at this stage a conservative. Longfield was actively supported by the Whigs, Lloyd, Sadleir and Whately. Whately and Sadleir would have stalled at pushing the candidature of a conservative. This view is corroborated by the events surrounding Longfield's successor in 1836. Whately was very involved in pushing the case of an unsuccessful candidate from 1832, the 'radical' Haig. Haig's opponent was Isaac Butt, a leading Tory. The clash between Haig and Butt led to an even clearer split between the Whigs and the Tories at the Board.

On 4 June 1836 Dr Franc Sadleir noted:

Election for Prof. of Pol. Economy deferred — McDonn(ell), Sandes and I for not electing Butt — rest for him.[26]

Sadleir, Sandes and McDonnell were all Whigs, whereas Butt's supporters were all Tories.

There was a head-on clash at the Board over the appointment, necessitating four Board meetings on 4, 18, 21 and 25 June before a final decision was taken. Prior's diary shows the stalemate that had emerged at the Board by 21 June:

21 June 1836
Full Board excepting Dr. Hodgkinson for purpose of electing a Professor of Political Economy but on the Bishop of Killaloe observing that he was of opinion the six Fellows present would be equally divided so that the Provost would be *annoyed* by determining — he therefore thought he should adjourn for a full Board.[27]

Prior indicates that the Archbishop was pushing Haig's case and the Provost, caught in the crossfire between the Tories and the Whigs at the Board, did not wish to have a casting vote. On 25 June Butt was elected Professor of Political Economy to succeed

Longfield when Dr Hodgkinson returned and joined to support his fellow Tories, Wall, Prior and Phipps.

25 June 1836
For Professorship of Political Economy ———— McDonnell, Sandes, Sadleir vote for Mr. Haig ————
for Isaac Butt, Wall, Prior, Phipps, the V. Provost, Hodgkinson; the provost refusing to vote.[28]

One can sense Prior's sense of delight at beating the Archbishop:

The Board of Trinity College elected Professor Butt as the most competent individual in this country to discharge the duties of the Professorship, and that, too, in direct opposition to the wishes and entreaties of his Grace.[29]

CONCLUSION

The Board's minutes and the two diaries of the Board members, Dr Thomas Prior and Dr Franc Sadleir, cast considerable light on the appointment of Mountifort Longfield and of his successor, Isaac Butt, to the chair of political economy at Trinity College. They indicate that the Board, contrary to the stated view, quickly agreed to Dr Whately's proposal for the chair.

However, some members of the Board objected to Whately's role in the selection process. This objection could have been based on the legitimate academic grounds that the founding of a chair does not give one the right to appoint the holder of the chair. However, Prior's diary shows that he objected to Whately interfering because he disagreed with the Archbishop's political views. Prior wanted a safe Tory in this new chair, a prospect he recognised would meet with the Archbishop's disfavour.

Political views seem to have played a major role in the selection of the first two holders of the chair. A Tory/Whig split on the Board emerged over the appointment of both Longfield and Butt. In the case of Butt the split was clear cut and the Tories won out in the end. In Longfield's case we can identify three Tories opposing his appointment with leading Whigs, including the Archbishop, supporting his case. This split indicates that Longfield was certainly not regarded by his Trinity colleagues as a conservative in 1832. Further evidence of Longfield's Whiggish political stance at this time may be adduced from his vote for North, a moderate Whig, rather than Lefroy, the High Tory, candidate in the parliamentary elections for the Trinity constituency in 1830.[30]

22

Mountifort Longfield's appointment

It must also be stressed that Longfield was the outstanding academic amongst the candidates, sufficiently so that he persuaded the diligent Dr Wall to cross party lines and vote for him.

Despite the political in-fighting on the appointment of holders of the chair, Trinity was fortunate in having as its first two professors of political economy two outstanding individuals, Mountifort Longfield and Isaac Butt.[31]

Notes

1. Mountifort Longfield, *Lectures on political economy* (Dublin, 1834). For a detailed analysis of Longfield's thought see R. D. C. Black, 'Mountifort Longfield: his economic thought and writings reviewed in relation to the theories of his times and of the present day', PhD thesis, TCD 1942; R. D. C. Black, *The economic writings of Mountifort Longfield* (New York, 1971); Lawrence Moss, *Mountifort Longfield: Ireland's first Professor of Political Economy* (Green Hill, 1976).

2. E. Jane Whately, *Life and correspondence of Richard Whately*, (London, 1866), pp 66-67, Vol. 1.

3. Report of the Address on the Conclusion of the first Session of the Dublin Statistical Society by Archbishop Whately, 19 June 1848.

4. Board Minutes, Trinity College 1832 (Manuscript Room, Trinity College).

5. William J. Fitzpatrick, *Memoirs of Richard Whately* (London, 1864), p. 180, Vol. 1.

6. *Ibid.*, p. 181.

7. Diary and Board Memoranda of Dr Thomas Prior, November 1826-July 1838 (Manuscript Room, Trinity College).

8. For the most recent assessment of Bartholomew Lloyd see R. B. McDowell and D. A. Webb, *Trinity College Dublin 1592-1952. An Academic History* (C.U.P. 1982), ch. 6.

9. Moss, *op. cit.*, p. 185.

10. Both Fitzpatrick and Whately's accounts are here reproduced: (1) 'The Provost at length consented, on condition that the Professor of Political Economy "should be of sound and safe Conservative views".' (*Memoirs of Richard Whately* by W. J. Fitzpatrick, London 1864). (2) 'The late Provost whose zeal and ardour in the cause of science were well known, told him that it had been suggested to him that, in the absence of any person having a full knowledge of the science, a person should be selected as the Professor of Political Economy who should be of sound and conservative views. He (Dr. Whately) was not a little appalled at such a suggestion, involving as it did the introduction of party politics into a subject of abstract science — party politics having about as much to do with Political Economy as they had with manufacture or agriculture. The matter was finally left to him, who consented that it should be so, on condition that he should submit certain questions with reference to the science, in writing, to the several candidates who were to reply under symbolical names; he being in perfect ignorance of the names of the candidates.' (Report of the Address on the Conclusion of the first Session of the Dublin Statistical Society by Archbishop Whately, 19th of June 1848).

11. R. B. D. McDowell, 'The journal of a disappointed man', Friends of the Library of Trinity College Dublin, *Annual Bulletin* (1954), pp 7-9. The author gives a brief account of Dr Prior's life and diaries.

12. Prior's diary, *loc.cit.*.

Antoin E. Murphy

13. See McDowell and Webb, *op.cit.* pp 157-159, for an analysis of the Tory views of this trio.

14. Prior's diary, *loc.cit.*

15. Board Minutes, *loc.cit.*

16. Prior's diary, *loc.cit.*

17. Whately, *Report to the Statistical Society, op.cit.*

18. Prior's diary, *loc.cit.*

19. For a list of his works, see J. B. Leslie, *Ferns clergy and parishes*, pp 26-27 (Dublin, 1936).

20. Rev. Henry Newland, *An examination of the evidence and arguments adduced by Dr. Doyle before the committee on tithes in Ireland*, (Dublin 1832) p. 4.

21. *Ibid.*

22. Prior's diary, *loc.cit.*

23. R. L. Meek has presented the view that Longfield was a political conservative. Longfield, along with Scrope and Read, is described as one of those who 'gave remarkably frank expression to the idea that political economy would have to be re-written from a new angle to make it suitable for consumption by the labouring classes' (*Studies in the labour theory of value*, (1956) pp 124-5, 2nd ed.). Meek repeats and reinforces this view in *Economics and ideology and other essays* (1967), classifying Longfield, along with Scrope and Read, as one whose fundamental approach 'was determined by a belief that what was socially dangerous could not possibly be true', p. 71. More recently Moss, *op.cit.*, while categorising Longfield as a harmony theorist, indicates that in his early years he was a political conservative. 'It is tempting to conclude . . . by stating that in his early years he was a political conservative intent upon defending the basic property relations of his society, and that towards the end of his life he became a liberal (or radical) reformer along the lines of Jeremy Bentham and (his contemporary) John Stuart Mill. This conclusion, while correct, obscures the essential unity of Longfield's economic thought and his place in the overall development of classical economic theory' (pp 180-1).

24. McDowell and Webb, *op.cit.*, p.152.

25. Beresford Papers (Manuscript Room T.C.D.), letter 51, February 1832. In this letter to Archbishop Beresford, Dr Wall alleged that Dr Prior favoured his two sons in the Scholarship examination of 1825. Of the eighty eight candidates who sat the examination twenty were awarded scholarships. However, Prior, who corrected a set of papers, only awarded one 'first best' and that to his younger son, and 'two second bests', one of which was to his elder son. Dr Wall was shocked by this because Prior's low marks adversely affected the results of many of the students who sat for the examination. He did not dispute that the younger son was worthy of Scholarship but felt that nepotism was involved in Prior's marking of the elder son's paper and in the overall return of marks which were completely out of line with those of other examiners.

26. Day Account Book of Franc Sadleir (Manuscript Room, T.C.D.) Mss F.6.19.

27. Prior's diary, *loc.cit.*

28. *Ibid.*

29. *Ibid.*

30. See Alan A. Tait, 'Mountifort Longfield 1802-1884; economist and lawyer', *Hermathena*, 133 (1982), p. 18.

31. For an evaluation of part of Isaac Butt's contribution to economic theory see Laurence S. Moss, 'Isaac Butt and the early development of the marginal utility theory of imputation', *History of Political Economy*, 5 (1973) pp 317-38.

O440
3120
Ireland

25-44

Landlords, bankers and merchants: the early Irish banking world, 1700-1820

by L. M. Cullen

Banking is in medieval parlance a 'mystery', relating not to the tangible evidence of possession but to the intangible question of how possession or activity is financed. If a man is at the wheel of a car, it is an incontrovertible fact; but how he financed the purchase of this expensive object, or indeed the question of his ownership at all, is in no sense self-evident. The question is certainly not easy to document, and, related to past possession, it is even more intangible. Hence the financing of investment has been explained both in marxist and capitalist theory on the evidence of a very meagre stock of known facts. It is merely a hypothesis in which the evidence has been re-arranged time and time again to support the fashionable theories of the day. The role of banks, for instance, was assumed forty years ago to be important in financing the Industrial Revolution: they were almost entirely eliminated from this role in the orthodoxy of the 1950s, and the wheel turning full circle, the drift of recent research has been on balance to see fruitful links between early banks and factory enterprises.

The ambiguity of the role of banks is of course paralleled in the ambiguity of the relationship of wealth to income, a thorny problem which arose long before high direct taxes led men to disguise income in various ways. The historian is frequently puzzled in case studies by the fact that the accumulation of wealth by a family over a period is usually larger than the evidence of income in the same years suggests to be possible. We rarely know enough on current account about income or expenditure or on capital account about saving and investment to make a coherent analysis, and the resources brought by windfalls (e.g. winning lottery tickets, inheritance or marriage), while they explain some features, are themselves equally hard to integrate into the long-term picture.

If the general question of how otherwise well-documented activities are financed poses usually insoluble problems, banking, related solely to these mysteries, must remain perforce the most obscure area of all in economic history. Even its nomenclature poses problems; some eighteenth-century figures indifferently described them-

25

selves or, were so described by contemporaries, as banker or merchant; others never attracted the title despite the nature of their activities. French 'banquiers' were rarely bankers in the sense, itself imprecise, in which the term was used in Ireland or Britain. Indeed, it is clear that the term was frequently applied in France to any person who handled an account for a merchant. What had bankers in common and what distinguished them from other figures? First, they were men who possessed wealth or the appearance of wealth. Alas for the would-be banker of no means, the presumption was important, and the quality of being presumed by the community to be wealthy or to have access to other people's wealth was itself of course a form of capital. The second feature which marked the banker off from merchants or from other users of the term banker lay in credit creation which was not simply incidental or even regular but characterised by a turn-over in credit, in whatever form created, which was a multiple of the capital employed in the business. In wealthy communities, credit creation (except for financial operations catering to the fiscal appetite of the state usually in the metropolis and often on a small scale except in war time) was less important than in poorer communities, as the diffusion of wealth reduced the centralised demand for credit and for credit instruments.

A consequence of centralisation was of course that the function of banking was peculiarly vulnerable to control or manipulation. This paper proposes to view Irish banking in terms of a promising early start whose subsequent development was compromised by a conflict of interest in which landlord demands for remitting prevailed over the merchant interest in discount. This conflict, it will be argued finally, was reflected later in an imperfectly integrated banking network in which the capital's role was an impaired one.

I.   PROMINENT IRISH DEBUT IN BANKING

The general rise in trade and industry across the eighteenth and early nineteenth centuries, with an inelastic supply of precious metals, was bound of course to lead eventually to the widespread emergence of banking. But what interests us here is what societies were precocious in developing banking outside metropolitan areas, and why? The two leaders were Scotland and Ireland, both of which had to cope with the stresses and strains of exceptional growth of

Landlords, bankers and merchants

trade and industry on a comparatively poor resource base and with no tradition of accumulated wealth.

In such conditions, men presumed wealthy turned to systematic credit creation quickly, and on the other hand the rest of the community faced with a shortage of the abundant specie of rich communities was well-disposed towards accepting credit creation in all its forms: notes in place of the familiar but sadly scarce specie, the intensive use of inland bills of exchange even for modest sums to finance activity. If London because of the massive gap between resources and demand in war-time pioneered metropolitan banking (itself a form of poverty, if you wish, compared with the solid flow of specie in both Paris and Amsterdam),[1] banking was slow to appear outside London and was only uncertainly drawn into an integrated national system.

Banking appeared at an earlier date in Ireland and Scotland than in provincial England, and this remains true even if Dublin and Edinburgh are excluded. But that of course is not realistic, because non-metropolitan banking presupposed a wider network. From its foundation in 1719 the bank of La Touche and Kane operated what was virtually a country-wide system of correspondents. Indeed we know more about Irish banking before 1750 than about English: perhaps an accident of sources, but on balance more a consequence of the early emergence of a system in Ireland. In the long term of course the development of banking owed more to Scotland than to any other country, because, though relatively poor it was led by its mineral resources and the talent of its people to finance an industrial revolution on a scale relatively as large as England's and almost as contemporaneously. Corporate banking, branch banking, cash credits, good office practices, are all the permanent Scottish contribution to modern banking. But before the 1760s Irish banking was more interesting than Scottish; a larger circulation of notes, more numerous locations, and the outline of a national credit structure.

In the eighteenth century the early financial prominence of both Irishmen and Scots was very evident. First, the greatest adventurers of the age were Irish and Scots: Law and Cantillon, Scot and Irishman respectively, represented it at its spectacular best or worst. In the 1760s the speculator, Sir George Colebrooke, who had married the heiress daughter of an Irish planter in the West Indies, occupied the seat of financial speculation in London. He drew heavily on the wealth of Irish families for his speculation: indeed as he seems to have tapped Catholic wealth as well as hard Protestant cash, his financial seduction was considerable as the two rarely combined. The London crisis of 1772 was largely the consequence of the convergence of two parallel streams of speculation: Colebrooke's financial circle on the one hand and on the other a Scottish group of speculators. Scots and Irish alike suffered disproportionately in the ensuing collapse, and indeed other interests in London were largely unhurt. In these years too Thomas Sutton was a rising figure in France. His interests were widespread; his place in speculative ventures was outstanding, reaching from the East Indies to Spain and the West Indies; and he was one of the prominent Parisian financiers of his day. Secondly, the networks of Irishmen and Scots were geographically diffuse. Scots and Irish, from economic backgrounds of limited opportunity, often moved far afield, and kinship as well as the requirements of trade thus made it easy for them to widen their contacts. Scots and Irish both represented the largest provincial groups from within the British Islands in London; they were established at an early date, and their financial interests in London were both distinctive and well defined, whereas correspondents from the outports or inland industrial centres were fewer or were subsumed into circles dominated by metropolitan interests. It is hardly surprising in these circumstances that they were the first provincials to set up banks in London. Coutts opened their London house in 1752, six years before the first London house set up by an English provincial banker,[2] and as befitted the more precocious Irish banking interests, Cairnes, Arthur, Cantillon, Hoare (Samuel) and Nesbitt had all appeared as bankers in London before the middle of the century. In Paris Scots banking was represented by the Alexanders and by Boyd Ker & Co. late in the century. The Irish presence in Paris was earlier and more sustained: Arthur, Cantillon, Loftus, Darcy, Woulfe and Waters provided a picture of seventy years of banking. The Hopes, Scots in Amsterdam, represented the pinnacle of Dutch private banking, and though the Herries were not bankers on the continent, their widespread commercial houses had close links with their bank in Britain, and represented a Scottish presence on the continent for which there was no English equivalent but which had been paralleled by Irish houses a generation earlier.

If the innovative genius of banking was purely Scottish from the 1770s, Scotland was in effect taking over a role in which innovation had been more on the Irish side before that. Even in the 1720s notes were circulating extensively: as Prior observed in 1729: 'were it not for bankers' notes which we have been passing in good plenty, it would be impossible to manage our domestic trade half so well as we do.'³ Indeed, some rough calculations of circulation, basing the combined issue on the known instances of some banks, would bear out Prior's surmise fully. If bank circulations equalled the stock of specie,⁴ Ireland's situation was unique at this stage, and proportionately note circulation in Dublin, easily the main centre of banking in Ireland, would have equalled or exceeded that in London. Moreover by 1752 banks either existed or had appeared at no less than seven centres outside Dublin; and at that stage Irish note circulation was double or treble the level of the 1720s.

The contraction in the note circulation in the early 1730s, which we know to have been very sharp both from the failure of the largest bank, Burton & Falkiner, in 1733 and the downturn in the circulation of La Touche & Kane,⁵ was the basis of Berkeley's interest in paper money. If bank paper contracted, there was no reason why it could not be artificially provided by a state institution and with results no less beneficial than those of banks in the 1720s. Cantillon's book which existed in manuscript by 1733 went more specifically into the nature of money, and has been hailed as the precursor of modern economic theory. Thus two of the first writers to approach the question of credit with sophistication and to analyse the nature of money were Irish. If Irish banking practice was advanced for its day it was only logical that Irish insights into theory should be also. Berkeley posed his questions in the light of the experience of Irish banking, and though Cantillon lived outside Ireland, his Irish links were numerous. The question that one must ask is why, if the Irish debut in banking was so original and innovative, it did not maintain its momentum? With hindsight of course it is clear that while Ireland like Scotland represented the effervescence of the fringe of the British Isles, its economic prospects could never have matched those of Scotland in the long term. But even if its prospects were poorer, one would have expected its banking to have fared better than it did. In fact banking in Ireland stagnated for forty years after its brilliant debut between 1720 and 1754, and not only did it stagnate but it did so in the midst of very rapid economic development. The combination of precocity with subsequent stagnation amid economic growth is so rare a phenomenon that it requires a very precise explanation. In reality of course no institution is totally stagnant. The replacement of specie by paper in the south was quite startling in the first two decades of the nineteenth century. Ireland adopted joint-stock banking earlier than England did; and later in the final quarter of the century the systematic use of the sub-branch as a means of gathering deposits in underpopulated or poor areas

29

was an Irish first, although it must be said that it was the only really novel feature in Irish banking in the second half of the nineteenth century.

II. LANDLORD INTEREST IN BANKING

The most widely held hypothesis about the origins of modern banking in the British Isles is that it grew out of the needs of merchants who required to discount paper to obtain working capital. But in fact discount in the strict sense was not a universal feature of early banking. In Dublin for instance there was no demand from its embryonic institutions for bills payable in the city; such bills were typically held by their possessors till maturity when their face-value was collected from the acceptor. Local paper did not pass through the banks as far as we can judge; provincial bills payable in Dublin remained an embarrassment; and bills on London which could be disposed of on the bill market (and to institutions) we know with more certainty were a much more common currency than bills drawn from London on Dublin which by definition had no further sale for exchange purposes and could be realised before maturity only by being hawked around because an effective discount market did not exist. The term discount for instance was scarcely used in the first half of the century though it came widely into vogue after 1760, although even then in a wide and loose use of the term. In London with its numerous institutions, many of them battening on the public finances, a discount or rediscount market could exist and even prosper. But in Ireland such government paper did not really exist before 1730, well after banking had already emerged and hence it was not a factor which nurtured banking into existence as in London and Paris. The growth of the public debt was erratic and the state never created short-dated paper. The only attraction of government finance was the prospect of access to cash held on the account of the state or more typically by a stake in the real but limited remitting of government money between different centres. A discount market in paper payable in Dublin is largely post-1800. While the discount market revolved almost exclusively around bills payable in Dublin by the 1870s, the bill of exchange had at that time ceased to be the mainstay of commercial banking.

In other words, transfer in space not in time was the main activity of Irish banking. Exchange was more important than discount, its practices were better-defined and were unambiguous. Although the bankers had recognised the discount element in exchange dealings

Landlords, bankers and merchants

by the 1720s, others may not have done so, or at least were unable to enforce a charge for discount until later in the century. The task of the banker was less the creation of credit than the transfer of surpluses: the matching of a surplus in the provinces or in Dublin against one in Dublin or in London respectively. In the process credit was of course created at two centres: the seller of paper received cash at the point of sale of the bill; the buyer received funds where he needed them. But this was achieved not in response to a shortage of capital but to a switch of credits and debits at two centres. The system economised cash in transit. Hence while it was universally resorted to in foreign trade in western Europe (and long before the period which concerns us), in inland payments it developed more quickly in poor countries than in rich countries where economic surpluses were readily available and specie more widely diffused. Indeed, in the initial stages, a high price was exacted for the service: bills were sold at a premium instead of at the almost universal discount of later times on bills on Dublin. Cash was often paid in before bills were available; this like the high exchange rates showed that remitting services were at a premium.

Banking did not therefore necessarily arise out of mercantile activity solely or exclusively. Because the Hoares were bankers in Cork in the 1720s at least in a general sense, it seems to have been assumed that they were bankers in the 1670s shortly after their establishment. If they were, they were the first bankers in Ireland, but the fact that in the 1710s they were still described as merchants removes any likelihood of a long banking pedigree. Indeed in Ireland, far from banking having originated in trade, it seems to have arisen from the need of the landlord classes to transfer rents, either from the country to Dublin, or from Dublin to London.[6] The main customers for bills in the less developed parts, and seasonally in bigger centres, were landowners. Rents were remitted in bills to Dublin into the hands of rent receivers of one sort or other. As rents were remitted as opportunity offered, and landlords only drew down their accounts over a longer period, these accounts were often in surplus. In the case of an absentee where the monies had to be remitted a stage further to London, they remained even longer in the account because remitting was often deferred in hope of securing a more advantageous exchange. The holders of these surpluses had the most substantial funds on the Dublin market, and the scale of remitting to absentees, roughly equal to the large favourable balance of trade, meant that they had a powerful place in the Dublin market for bills on London. The importance of the Cairnes, among the first

31

of Irish bankers, reveals how widespread this remitting business was. In addition to being based in Dublin and London, a member of the family had even been a banker in Limerick, possibly the first bank outside the capital, and the only known provincial 'branch' of a Dublin bank in the eighteenth century.[7] Limerick was a very minor port, but its inland situation made it the focal centre of the landlord rents of three counties and of part of a fourth (Kerry). In the inland business of another banking house, Limerick ranked with Cork in importance.[8] The first recognisable Irish bankers, the houses of Burton and Cairnes, grew out of such remitting. Both houses, it should be added, were established by sons of landed families. Coming from Clare and Donegal/Monaghan respectively, they reflected the interest that country gentry had in rent-receiving in Dublin. The landed dimension is thus very evident in early Irish banking just as in Scotland, banking in a landlord city, Edinburgh, preceded that in the mercantile city Glasgow.

The first true merchant banks emerged only at the end of the 1710s and the 1720s. The partnership of La Touche & Kane began in 1719, and the house of Swift was opened in 1722. Not only did true merchant banks emerge late, but some of the merchant banks themselves evolved over time into landlord banks. This was most evident in the case of La Touche's house which switched from mercantile associations to landed and even aristocratic ones from mid-century or even before. The house of Swift in time went the same way, becoming the bank of Newcomen in the second half of the century. Finlay's bank, mercantile in origin also went in the same direction and within a few years of its establishment. These moreover were the sole three banks which survived from the banking boom of the 1750s till the end of the century. Landlords themselves founded banking businesses: the house of Gardiner & Hill is the most obvious instance, benefitting from Gardiner's office as deputy vice-treasurer, having the powerful figure of Lord Bessborough associated with it at one stage. Nathaniel Clements, teller of the exchequer under Gardiner, taking the business over when they withdrew in 1737, played a similar role in the 1740s and 1750s. As agent for the pensioners he remitted monies and he also transferred funds on army account. His links were close with the houses of Mitchell and Dawson. In 1758 Clement's business was turned unwisely into the house of Malone, Clements & Gore, in some respects the most singular banking experiment of the eighteenth century, run by three M.P.s including the chancellor of the exchequer. When it collapsed in 1759 it brought down the houses of

Landlords, bankers and merchants

Dawson and Mitchell. But Mitchell's house was reopened quickly. It was much larger than meets the eye; it handled the accounts of many landlords, and had the largest remitting turnover of any Irish house in the 1760s and 1770s. Its success in the 1760s and 1770s and the extent of its connections provides ample food for thought. Two lesser remitting houses, Birch and Underwood, handling rent remittances but little other business, also emerged: all three thrived in a period when rents roughly doubled. Apart from these houses, only two banks emerged in Dublin between 1760 and 1793, the year in which John Claudius Beresford, a son of the arrogant first revenue commissioner, opened a bank. One of these two banks, Colebrooke's bank in 1764, was largely a venture to remit money abroad to finance speculation on the London market. In fact banking between 1763 and 1793 was dominated to a remarkable extent by the activity of rent remitters and landlords. This is particularly evident in Dublin where the sole merchant venture was founded by Coates, a Quaker, and Lawless, the convert son of a Catholic wool merchant. In the rest of the country outside Cork, excepting two small banks, one in Waterford,[9] and the other in Belfast, not a single bank was opened until 1789 when the landlord bank of Maunsell was launched in Limerick. In Cork, where the merchant thrust was so evident in the first half of the century, the impetus to banking was remarkably weak. The house of Pike, opened in 1771, was in effect a reconstitution of the Quaker business of Hoare but on a smaller scale. The merchant bank of Hewitt was a short-lived venture. For what was one of the major ports of Europe with an enormous turnover in bills, the scale of merchant initiative in this period was startlingly small. The two pre-1760 houses of Travers and Falkiner were metamorphosed into houses with heavy landlord involvement in their direction, and the house of Tonson or Warren established in 1768 was a pure landlord venture with no less than five members of parliament associated with it at one time or other.

Just as the Cork bankers drew on the capital and management talent of the gentry, the Dublin banks, increasingly identified with the gentry, did likewise. In 1782 Robert Alexander, a nephew to the member for Londonderry, was a partner in Newcomen's bank, and Richard Neville, like Arthur Jones Neville before him, was a partner in Finlay's bank.[10] Likewise, Arthur Dawson was a banker in Dublin, married to a niece of Lord Tyrone, a Beresford. John Claudius Beresford's venture into banking in 1793 thus had family antecedents. Between 1797 and 1804, when inflation gave a new impetus to banking, the Colcloughs in Wexford, Talbot at Malahide, the Frenchs at Tuam, and Langrishe in Kilkenny, were improbable sources of banking, just as Thomas Lighton who had made a fortune in India and had become a baronet and member of Parliament was a partner in the new Dublin bank opened in 1798. Landed bankers were closely identified with politics, a field in which their ascent was made easier by the indebtedness of grandees to them. In the 1773 parliament there were five bankers plus two men with a banking future. The 1782 parliament had no less than ten members of banking enterprises, plus a future banker and the son of a banker. Eight members of families with present or future banking connections sat in the 1791 parliament. Political associations were immensely important to rising or aspiring bankers. Not only did sycophancy to the great bring custom, but political contacts brought government accounts to the bankers. From an early date, landlord-related bankers such as, for instance, Hugh Henry in the 1730s remitting money on government account attracted government funds into their coffers. Luke Gardiner, deputy vice-treasurer in the 1720s and Clements, teller of the exchequer who stepped into the shoes of Gardiner & Hill, had the use of government money. The banking activity of Gardiner or of Clements were the most blatant cases of this activity, stemming from within the treasury itself, and only the victory of the political grandees over the executive in 1755 made it possible to carry this experiment a stage further into a bank containing the chancellor of the exchequer. When this bank failed in 1759, the Duke of Bedford was able to exert the central authority sufficiently to extract a promise from the partners not to engage further in banking.[11] This was consecrated in an act of that session, which prohibited banking by people who held public offices.[12] Its passage reflected the temporary political eclipse that followed economic problems. But the act proved ineffective, because once public money left the exchequer it could still be used for banking purposes. Clements' associate, Mitchell, and in time Clements' own son were to engage in such activity. Hugh Henry Mitchell in the 1770s was treasurer to the Barracks Board and in the 1780s Clements' son, Henry Theophilus, was an army agent moving large sums of money on army account. Such funds were an enormous advantage to bankers such as Mitchell or Clements. Landlords had cash in the provinces but required it in the capital for use there or for conversion into bills on London. The Barracks Board had funds in Dublin but required cash at barrack locations throughout the country. Thus a banker with access to both landlord and government finance was extremely liquid. It also made it easy for him to act as an agent for provincial bankers: Clements was the Dublin correspondent of the powerful Cork landlord bank of Falkiner, Leslie & Kellett, the oldest surviving bank in Cork, landlord-dominated and politically well-connected.

The Irish gentry were extremely powerful. Roughly 2,000 families held about 20% of the national income. Even if they were not absentee, the estates of landed gentry, as a result of formation in or by plantation, had not grown organically. Widely scattered, rents from them had to be remitted to Dublin. The richest landowner of his time, speaker Conolly, lived at Castletown but drew the bulk of his rent from Donegal. About a quarter of the rents went to absentees, not including others who frequently sojourned at Bath. The Irish gentry were individually richer than the Scottish (2,000 families compared with 6,000, many on compact estates in the Lowlands). Hence the gentry were a more dominant influence on banking than in Scotland, and in contrast to Scotland where Edinburgh after the 1750s had to share its place in banking with Glasgow, the sharp rise in landlord rents from mid-century made it possible for a rich gentry to overshadow mercantile banking to an unprecedented degree. Dublin in consequence was a capital without a financial class. The confused politics of the 1719 proposal for a national bank show this, because the coterie of landed supporters of the project who attracted merchant support were defeated, The Bank of Ireland in 1783 reflects the same situation. Its major investors were all gentry or peers: no less than four La Touches put up the maximum investment permitted, and a La Touche was governor for the first nine years. Not a single one of the rich merchants of post-1760 Dublin excepting Lawless and Coates made the transition to banking.

III. MERCHANTS IN BANKING

The previous merchant involvement in banking itself had not been progressive. It had been most evident in two periods, the 1720s and the late 1740s and early 1750s. Both were periods when bills were in brisk demand; the favourable and usually large balance of trade was greatly reduced; and the exchanges plummetted.[13] In the 1720s exports stagnated, while imports, because of rising grain and wine imports, failed to contract in the prevailing depression. In the second period, the greatest boom in Irish history, imports soared even more rapidly than rising exports. In the two periods, wine, a major item in landlord expenditure especially in periods when rents

35

rose sharply as they did in the 1720s and again in the late 1740s, was a significant item in imports. With the exchanges under pressure merchants were eager to find bills to pay for imports, and hence set up houses to compete with the established banks. In the 1720s at least three of the Dublin houses were merchant ones; Cork merchants, selling London bills through Dublin agents to a less extent than before, and disposing of them to remitters on the spot in County Cork, were in the process of becoming bankers, a fact illustrated even in efforts to remit money for London from Dublin to Cork. The late forties and early fifties were the heyday of merchant banking in Irish history. First, merchants were the majority of bankers for the first time. Whereas only three of the Dublin banks in the 1720s were mercantile, no less than six of eight banks were in 1754. Second, merchants banks were larger than the other houses. They expanded their purchase of bills by the issue of notes, and the Quaker house of Willocks & Dawson in 1754 had the huge circulation of £212,000, the largest known circulation of an Irish private bank before the 1790s.[14] Non-merchant houses were much more cautious; they sought to acquire bills for their account-holders rather than to meet the cash needs of expanding trade. In other words they sought bills primarily to meet the demands of landed customers, whereas merchant banks, meeting trade demands as well as landed needs, sought to purchase bills ever more extensively, confident that they could pass them on to importers as well as to rent remitters. As rents were rising and hence the size of remittances, the competition for bills on London was intense. Landlord bankers were noticeably less expansive than other banks. Their known circulations were usually smaller. Some of the houses never issued notes; others showed a tendency to get out of note issue entirely. Significantly, one of the criticisms of the Irish banks by a committee of the Irish House of Commons in 1756 was that their note issue greatly exceeded the capital of the houses,[15] a criticism which is less telling than it sounds because a business handling bills was highly liquid, and turnover would greatly exceed capital in any normal event. Significantly, most of the banks founded at this time outside Dublin also were merchant ones: two seem to have emerged in Cork, two in Galway and one in Belfast. Moreover, the new banking was non-conformist in the sense that it was frequently in the hands of Catholics, Quakers or Presbyterians rather than Anglicans. One of the Dublin banks was Catholic, one Quaker and a third with the Roscommon family of French involved was from outside the charmed circle of the Anglican gentry. The two Galway banks were

Catholic; the founder of one of them turned Protestant in 1748 on his death bed; this was less likely to have been because of fear in life of losing his Catholic clients as a Dublin paper suggested[16] than in the interest of safeguarding his succession from the penal laws.

Banking was passing out of the hands of the established gentry in the 1750s, and in a small measure out of the reach of the capital itself. The problems experienced by Clements and his backers in the 1750s, the curious not to say desperate expedient represented by the house of Malone, Clements & Gore in 1758 and its failure along with that of the closely related house of Mitchell in 1759, all point to a gentry banking crisis whose course and politics have yet to be fully teased out. Its course, I think, relates less to the state of the economy than to specific problems of the banking gentry themselves. Clements' financial problems were attributed to his giving up the post of teller for the post of deputy vice-treasurer.[17] But this cannot be true. It was precisely the latter post which made possible the banking operations of Luke Gardiner and it was under the umbrella of Gardiner that Clements in turn had conducted his own banking operation. Moreover, it is hard to see why Clements would have exchanged one post for the other post if it was destined to deprive him of access to government cash. Clements seems to have continued banking operations. What happened was an outcome of a combination of circumstances which were not foreseen: an otherwise compliant Lord Lieutenant's opposition to banking based on public monies, and the determination of the new teller, a relative of the Lord Lieutenant, to employ the exchequer surplus in lending on the security of mortgages.[18] These circumstances drove Clements into dependence on other banks and ultimately into the 1758 venture. The interdependence of the Clements interest and of the houses of Dawson and Mitchell put the whole coterie on the road to collapse. The fact that of the five houses which failed in 1754-55 three were Catholic and one — the largest — Quaker made it easy for the political establishment, riding high in political influence but now deprived of a ready flow of public money to underpin its banking operation, to take steps in some desperation against its commercial rivals. The act of 1756, passed at the nadir point of the banking fortunes of the banking gentry, prohibited merchants from conducting a banking business.

For all practical purposes the act brought merchant banking to an end. Despite the phenomenal growth of Irish trade and industry a single banking house was opened in Dublin between 1760 and 1797 by individuals with a mercantile background; that of Lawless and Coates. In the provinces, if Pike's bank is excepted, the bank of Rivers in Waterford was the only bank (with no previous antecedents) to have a long history: Hewitts in Cork was an inauspicious enterprise, as were the two Belfast banks which appeared in 1787 and 1789. In fact, the note issue contracted in the 1760s, falling well below the level of the 1750s. In 1754 the note issue was probably the equal of the supply of specie; in 1797, even including the circulation of the Bank of Ireland, it was one fourth. Merchant origins were prejudicial to bankers. John Bagwell, originally a flour miller in Clonmel, had to suffer the epithet of Marshall Sacks (a play on the name of the celebrated general of the time Maréchal Saxe). Mussenden, Adair & Bateson in Belfast brought their banking partnership to an end in 1757; and Lawton, Carleton & Feray in Cork who continued a note issue failed in 1760. It was in fact open to other houses to do as Lawton, Carleton & Feray did — to continue to issue notes by ceasing to describe themselves as bankers — but none did. It is quite clear that note issues generally were distrusted, and, so far as they were tolerated, were less acceptable in the hands of merchants than of other houses. Distrust of notes increased at the end of 1759. What is most interesting is the emergence of merchant discount houses in the late 1780s and early 1790s. The term discount house was not common parlance in England or Ireland; such houses did not issue notes, but they kept regular hours of opening as did bankers, and they were an effort by merchants to enter into the market to sell and buy bills outside the limited confines of the merchant community. In the provinces this development was confined to Belfast (1785) and Galway (1795), both towns with disappointed banking ambitions. Moreover, Galway was the focal centre of the largest network of Catholic landed and trading families in the kingdom, and Belfast was the bastion of Presbyterian radicalism. It is no accident that Waddell Cunningham, whose ambition was for a Belfast independent of Dublin finance, was a partner both in the Belfast discount house of 1785 and in the second of the two Belfast banks. The two Galway discount houses, it should be noted, eventually combined in a bank.

In Dublin the dimensions of the bill business of several merchant houses pointed to a wish to enter banking. The house of the Galway man John Blake, which petered out in the early 1780s, the business of Joshua & Joseph Pim who rose to prominence in the same decade, and the house of Robert Shaw with a large turnover, and the Dublin agency of four provincial bankers are the clearest instances. None of these houses turned into banks, though Shaw's did, after all mercantile business had been wound up, opening in 1798 under the magic name of a partner Sir Thomas Lighton who through Indian wealth had acquired both land and a seat in parliament. Indeed existing bankers did not like the Bank of Ireland, the politics of whose foundation and early years are quite complex. John Finlay, for instance, was described in 1782 as 'opposed as much as possible [to] the establishment of the National Bank'.[19] The price paid for the bankers' support was that they dominated the Bank. Even years before, the Government leanings of David La Touche had been quoted: '[would] willingly serve Government but he has an eye to popularity as it might be of use to his shop'.[20] In fact, of course, as the Bank was to hold the accounts of the state, thus perpetuating the old gentry tradition of using public money, it was amenable to the wishes of government, and the bankers of the period were supporters of government, or mere nominal opponents. The La Touche and government weight combined effectively silenced the merchant interest among the early directors. The Bank's turnover in discounts expanded very slowly before the government finances fell into deficit in the course of the 1790s. Moreover, it had begun with excessive caution: its role in the depression of 1783-4 was ingloriously restrictive.

IV. BREAKDOWN OF OLD AND GENESIS OF MODERN SYSTEM

Indeed this conservative and geographically narrow banking system not only revolved around specie but did so to a greater extent than it had previously. Despite the existence of banking in the south, a very large volume of guineas was dispatched from Dublin to the provinces, and one of the roles of a provincial banker was to ensure a wide enough margin between his bill drawings on Dublin and the negotiation of bills on the Dublin market to finance these consignments. In other words at the end of the 1780s there was rather little difference between the south and north where banking scarcely existed and where the circulation of guineas is better-known because of what happened at the end of the 1790s. One must ask at this point why, when paper began to recover ground in the south after 1797, guineas remained the medium of exchange in the north. That this occurred is usually taken as a fact of life, either not meriting comment or at least not lending itself to intelligent commentary. The north, remote socially and, outside the linen enclave around Belfast, economically backward, had great problems in remitting, and northern gentry from an early date had a close association with banking in Dublin and London. The Cairnes both in Dublin and London were the first instance of northern bankers, followed by Gardiner & Hill, Richard Dawson, later by Clements and a coterie of Sneyds and Nesbitts, finally by Sir Annesley Stewart and Alexander. These families came predominantly from the south and west of the province. A dichotomy existed between the commercially active and Presbyterian Belfast region and the poorer and landlord-dominated reaches of the rest of the province. There was thus a real tension between two distinct milieus in the north. Belfast was already keen in the early 1780s to break its dependence on Anglican Dublin, but despite the fact that the influential figure of Waddell Cunningham lent his weight to this aspiration and was also a party to one of the two banking ventures, the effort at least in banking was timid. The powerful gentry group, whose position could not be openly challenged, was able to make an archaic insistence on the payment of guineas after 1797. They were little involved in trade or industry: unlike their southern counterparts, they invested relatively little in the linen industry which in the north prospered in the hands of Presbyterian or non-conformist drapers and bleachers. In the south on the other hand many of the gentry had been drawn into industry or marketing to some extent. Although banking was predominantly gentry and conservative, its character was quite different from that of the northern banking interest. For one thing, the southern gentry bankers whose banking interest lay in the south and not in the capital itself were somewhat less obsessed with remitting than were the northern gentry. None of them had a stake in Dublin banking, and the one Corkman who had gone to the banking world — Samual Hoare in 1744 to London — had been a Quaker. Indeed, in reverse one of the Dublin Pims was a partner in the Cork house of Pike in the 1770s. Significantly, too, provincial banking encountered the problem of Dublin banking exclusiveness: it is noteworthy that the Dublin accounts of the major Munster banks were at one time or other handled by non-banking houses: four were serviced by Shaw including the house of Falkiner, Leslie & Kellet for whom Clements had acted in the 1780s. Secondly, some of the southern gentry had had recent involvement in industry or trade, and one of the original partners in Warren's bank, Jeffereyes, had been an industrial promoter on a grand scale at Blarney. Thirdly, Cork's trades, predominantly in provisions, were more speculative than the north's, and insistence on guineas would have been more impractical than in the north and less in the gentry's own immediate interest, given the wild fluctuations in prices. A

Landlords, bankers and merchants

rigid insistence on guineas would have led to immediate problems in payments. In the north it succeeded only because the spread of cotton around Belfast halted or reversed the drift of linen to Belfast, and preserved elsewhere in the province an archaic and static market structure for another two decades.

If continued payment in specie in the north after 1797 is an exceptional feature in the story of Irish banking, equally so is the contrast between the conservative and timid path of banking in Ireland and the evidence of initiative in banking and speculation by Irishmen abroad. Of course, there were very different groups involved in banking even within Ireland. If a powerful Anglican group divided between the north and Dublin is an obvious force, another was the west of Ireland interest, Catholic or part Catholic, evident first in the appearance of two banking houses in Galway itself in the first half of the century, and in the opening both of Dillons and of a Dublin house with a Roscommon partner in the 1750s; and later in the near-banking activity of John Blake and in the opening of two discount houses in Galway in 1795 with banking to follow. Over the century this group waned, but it had represented a force drawing on merchants and the merchant-related gentry of the west, which might have blossomed in different circumstances. Abroad, Irish Catholics did so in fact.

It is often assumed that banking abroad related to the needs of the state. Superficially it did, of course. The Paris notarial records are quite literally barren of mention of a bill of exchange, but that is simply because Paris notarial practices were different from French provincial ones, and bill protests were not made before notaries. In reality the Paris bankers were neither simply Jacobite nor court bankers. Richard Cantillon had a huge turn-over of bills of exchange, which are easily followed in the activity of his Nantes correspondents, the MacNamara brothers. Woulfe and Waters did a large business in Paris. Patrick Darcy, a banker in the 1760s, was a partner of Thomas Sutton de Clonard both in mining and East Indian ventures. Significantly, Sutton's empire, created by marriage alliances, was eventually to include the MacCarthies in Bordeaux, Andrew French in London, and Edward Byrne in Dublin. Byrne was to become the richest Dublin merchant of the late eighteenth century. Sutton died in 1782 prematurely. But the celebrated *Caisse d'escompte* grew out of the circle around him, and it is not fanciful to see the popularisation of the term discount house in Ireland as in some way related to the same concerns and to the actual institution.

41

Much money moved between London and Paris. Not only did Jacobites and wandering Georgian landowners require rents remitted to them but France too channelled a large portion of its payments abroad, especially those to the east, through London: bills both on London and Paris were therefore in demand. As English trade with France was relatively small, and for much of the century seems to have been smaller than the Irish trade with France whose payments were channelled through London, the trade between France and Ireland provided the largest and most concentrated volume of paper in the business. It was access to this as much as their Jacobite and court contacts that gave the Irish bankers such a prominent role. It was in many ways a remitting business. Provincial houses in France drew on accounts with Paris bankers, and these accounts were financed either by bills on Paris remitted from London or by bills which the Irish traders in the French provinces or in Ireland drew on London. However, this activity had its speculative side, most evident in the case of Cantillon. But even in his case it did not revolve solely around public finances. His brother Bernard was recruiting Irishmen and Frenchmen alike for a Louisiana colony in 1718. Sutton proposed a somewhat similar venture as late as 1760. Sutton's circle is arresting because it is one which invested in mines and East Indian trade and whose needs related even more to the financing of private activity than to the passive remitting of money. Sutton's influence was even evident in Ireland. John Howard Kyan, his son-in-law, a small county Wexford landowner, was mining in Co. Wicklow in the 1780s and even received a grant from the Irish parliament.

The nature of Dublin banking in the 1780s with its emphasis on remitting meant that beyond the superficial ease of remitting at national level an integrated banking system did not exist. The Irish banking framework as an entity began to collapse after 1797. In the north payment in specie was rigidly insisted on to the benefit of northern landlords but to the detriment of Dublin merchants who saw Belfast independence beginning to take practical shape for the first time. In the extreme south, note issues, especially in the hands of bankers in the provisioning trades, represented the first instance outside the big cities of the almost total replacement of specie by notes. The collapse of Munster banking in 1820 is in part a reflection of its unhealthy dependence on provisioning. In the north banking had not developed at all: the two small banks of the 1780s had closed. When banking reappeared on a small scale in 1808-9, it responded to the long-felt aspirations of Presbyterian merchants around Belfast to break their dependence on Dublin. Hence in fact when banking burgeoned in the 1820s and 1830s it was based heavily on a narrow circle of merchants in Belfast, had few ties with Dublin and excluded the gentry. The rapidity with which Ireland adopted joint-stock banking in the 1820s is easy to explain. Unlike England there were no vested interests standing against it. Munster banking had virtually collapsed, and the north, because more than in any other province the Anglican gentry had dominated its life, had no internal banking traditions at all. It was of course inevitable that Irish banking would tend to centre on London. But it did so to a larger extent than was necessary because of purely political and social forces which had weakened or prevented the rise of a real discount market in Dublin. While the Bank of Ireland was tied to Dublin by its charter, the two great institutions of southern banking, the National and the Provincial, were to establish their head-offices in London. By contrast, the three Belfast banks not only held their head offices in Ireland, but in Belfast. Two Dublin banks also opened their head offices in Ireland: the Royal which as constituted in 1836 really grew out of the circle around the Dublin Quakers, and the Hibernian, nationalist and politically non-conformist. Moreover, in the nineteenth century, as the lack of an Irish parliament shifted the focus of gentry attention to London, the Dublin merchants began to assume a more effective role within Dublin banking institutions. The Royal and the Belfast banks too, it is clear, held much of their investment in local stocks until the 1880s. It is important to appreciate that the banking system was shaped not only by the economic forces of the nineteenth century but by institutional and political obstacles which were unique in Europe and which were in essence an inheritance from the eighteenth century. Such was the power of these forces that early daring in practice and precocious insight in theory bore little fruit after a promising dawn in the first half of the eighteenth century.

Notes

1. French banks did not issue bearer notes as a significant form of currency, and the Bank of Amsterdam's bank money represented a form of deposit receipt.

2. J. M. Price, *France and the Chesapeake* (Ann Arbor, 1973), i, 621. See also L. S. Pressnell, *Country banking in the industrial revolution* (Oxford, 1956), pp 117-18.

3. T. Prior, *Observations on coin in general* (Dublin, 1729), p. 45.

4. An assumption which Berkeley broadly made. See *The Querist* in J. Johnston, *Bishop Berkeley's Querist in historical perspective* (Dundalk, 1970), p. 127, query no. 33.

5. See Abstract ledger of La Touche and Kane, 1726-1743, Allied Irish Banks, Dublin.

L. M. Cullen

6. L. M. Cullen, 'Merchant communities overseas, the navigation acts and Irish and Scottish responses', in L. M. Cullen and T. C. Smout, eds. *Comparative aspects of Scottish and Irish economic and social history 1600-1900* (Edinburgh, 1977), p. 173.

7. Genealogical Office, National Library, Dublin, MS 170, pp 57-66. Cairnes died in 1725.

8. Abstract ledgers of La Touche and Kane, National Library, MS 2785: 1719-1726; Allied Irish Banks: 1726-1743.

9. Assuming that the bank of Newport was in existence in 1760, or came into being shortly afterwards.

10. G. O. Sayles, 'Contemporary sketches of the members of the Irish parliament in 1782', *Proceedings of the Royal Irish Academy*, vol. 56, section c, no. 3, 250, 272. Banking experience thus gave authority to the observations in Arthur Jones Nevill's *Some hints on trade, money and credit, humbly addressed to the true friends of Ireland* (Dublin, 1762).

11. Public Record Office, London, SP63/416/257-8, Duke of Bedford to Pitt, 25 Dec. 1759.

12. 33 George II, c. 14, s.xv. Malone's loss of the chancellorship of the exchequer was another feature.

13. i.e. using modern parlance. Contemporaries quoted the Irish exchanges as the surplus of Irish pounds acquired by £100 sterling. Hence favourable movements for the Irish pound were expressed as a 'fall', and adverse movements as a 'rise'.

14. L. M. Cullen, *Anglo-Irish Trade 1660-1800* (Manchester, 1968), pp 199n, 200.

15. *Irish Commons Journal*, v, 378.

16. *Faulkner's Dublin Journal*, 6 August 1748.

17. See Charles O'Hara, Memorandum on Co. Sligo. Public Record Office of Northern Ireland, T.2812/19.

18. It is hoped to publish a fuller account of this episode.

19. G. O. Sayles, *art. cit.*, 256.

20. M. Bodkin, 'Notes on the Irish parliament in 1773', *Proceedings of the Royal Irish Academy*, vol. 43, section C, no. 4, 205.

0440
3120
France
0322
45-74

Richard Cantillon – an Irish banker in Paris

by Antoin E. Murphy

Richard Cantillon's *Essai sur la nature du commerce en général* was posthumously published in France in 1755.[1] However, in order to understand the background against which it was written it is necessary to move back from the Enlightenment period to the years 1715-20. Then France, greatly impoverished by the reign of Louis XIV, under the direction of the Scotsman John Law, embarked on an ambitious macroeconomic experiment. Richard Cantillon, an increasingly influential banker in Paris, witnessed the genesis, growth and destruction of this eighteenth century experiment, frequently referred to as Law's System or the Mississippi System.

Cantillon, however, was more than a passive witness for he acted as a business partner with John Law at the start of the System and as a 'bear' of Mississippi shares at its apogee. During the System Cantillon made a fortune but his enjoyment of this money was greatly curtailed by the legal purgatory he experienced arising from his Mississippi related profits. Cantillon was both enriched and scarred by Law's System. 'Monetary theories arise out of monetary disturbances.'[2] It is the contention of this paper that the monetary environment of France between 1715-20 conditioned Cantillon's views on monetary theory. Cantillon in the *Essai* was somewhat circumspect in his attack on Law's System directing his argument not *ad hominem* against Law or the Mississippi System but rather against the view that monetary and exchange rate policy could be used to achieve desirable macroeconomic objectives. As such because the *Essai* does not concentrate on specific contemporary difficulties it transcends the problems of the eighteenth century and remains a relevant and readable work in the twentieth century.

The French environment of 1715-20 is not totally alien to the twentieth century debate between Keynesianism and Monetarism. John Law was greatly concerned by the underutilization of resources in France. He believed that a complete change in the monetary system was required involving the demonetization of specie and its replacement with paper credit. Furthermore, he wanted to pursue an expansionary monetary policy which would push the interest rate down to 2 per cent.

45

Antoin E. Murphy

Richard Cantillon banked in Paris during the System and wrote the *Essai* after it collapsed. In it he points out the way changes in both the money supply and exchange rate can have short term benefits on employment and output and long term repercussions in terms of inflation and balance of payments deficits. He was against excessive financial innovation because he felt that ultimately it had a corrupting influence on politicians. They started using the System for their own ends and when the public became suspicious the system exploded.

This paper is divided into three sections. The first section discusses Cantillon's background and his introduction to banking in Paris between 1714-1716; the second outlines Law's System; the third deals with Cantillon's activities during Law's System and summarises the macroeconomic division of opinion that emerged between Cantillon and Law.

I

Richard Cantillon was born in Ballyronan, in the parish of Bally-heigue, County Kerry. Unfortunately, we do not have the date of his birth but we have shown that the attribution of a date of birth of 16 March 1697 to him by Joseph Hone is incorrect.[3] Richard Cantillon was certainly not a child prodigy operating in the banking world of the eighteenth-century France as Hone would have us believe.[4] We would conjecture, from a detailed genealogical study of his family roots, that he was born sometime around 1680.

One of the benefits of tracing Richard Cantillon's genealogy is that we now know that his maternal grandmother, Jane Arthur, was the sister of Sir Daniel Arthur. Sir Daniel Arthur was a merchant and banker and it is believed that it was primarily through him rather than the Chevalier Richard Cantillon that the economist was introduced to the world of banking.

As far as can be ascertained Daniel Arthur was knighted by James II in 1690 while this monarch was in Ireland.[5] Arthur, it may be surmised, was acting as a banker for the Jacobites, a business that became increasingly lucrative as the Irish Jacobites emigrated to the Continent taking specie and portable assets with them and needing the services of a banker. Indeed prior to the attack on Limerick, and the Treaty which ended hostilities on Irish soil between the warring factions, the Marquis d'Albyville, writing

The speculative brazier of Mississippi stock being stirred by John Law. A satirical print in Mémoires de la Régence (Paris, 1729).

from Limerick, shows the extent of Arthur's deposit taking activities from the Irish Jacobites:

I believe the King of France would perform a great act of justice in carrying out an inventory of the assets of all those people who have withdrawn from Ireland to France, which could be done through the threat of the death penalty and confiscation of their assets; that all those French or Irish merchants and bankers, who have Irish assets under their control, would be obliged to declare them and to employ a third or a half for the defence of their country. One would find a considerable amount of wealth, a large amount of it stolen from the King. The Parisian banker, the Chevalier Arthur, will be found to have close to 2 million livres of their wealth in his possession; and others in Nantes and in St. Malo, in Brest and in other French ports. Never has a kingdom been pillaged to such an extent as this one over the last two years; the desolation is beyond description due to the lack of discipline and conduct by the officers on the general staff.[6]

The attribution of 2 million French pounds — over £150,000 sterling at the prevailing exchange rate — in Irish assets held by Arthur on the continent may seem excessive. Was it not poetic licence on the part of d'Albyville to attribute such a large sum to Arthur? After all the Irish coinage was estimated never to have exceeded £300,000 for any one year in the seventeenth century.[7] Whilst d'Albyville's account may be somewhat exaggerated the very fact that he was prepared to mention such a large sum is indicative of the dominating importance of Arthur's bank in Irish Jacobite affairs.

Arthur was certainly multi-national in his trading and banking operations. He lived in London, banked in both London and Paris and died in Spain. Documents relating to his banking business show that he was one of the most prominent bankers of his day. In 1712, for example, we find his Parisian agent furnishing the great French financier Crozat with a letter of credit for £40,000 sterling on M. Arthur of London.[8] His Parisian agent was the Chevalier Richard Cantillon, an older second cousin of Richard Cantillon, the economist. One final piece of evidence shows the immense wealth of Sir Daniel Arthur. In 1729 the Earl of Egmont observed in his diary that a Mr Bagnall had, through his marriage to Sir Daniel Arthur's widow, obtained a fine collection of paintings:

I would not omit that this morning Mr Bagnall shewed me a great number of very fine original paintings, which he got by marriage with the Lady Arthur, widow of Sir Daniel Arthur, a rich Irish merchant who died in Spain. There is a fine large piece of Vandyke for which he asks 400l., it is Diana and Endymion. There are two large pieces of Rubens, one, the Legend of St. Martin cutting off a piece of his cloke to relieve the beggar,

Richard Cantillon — an Irish banker in Paris

there are several figures in it as big as life. [There is also a very fine landscape, large, of the same master: a landscape by Artois, the figures by Teniers. Six or seven pictures of this last master, four of which match and represent the different parts of the day, several pieces of Monglio, a famous painter in Spain, little known here, together with his own picture. He was fond of painting cupids. Beatrix Constanza, Dutch(ess) of Loraine, a full length by Vandyke, and some other portraits of his, a fine preserved piece of Castle and birds by Savary and divers of the Brugels, some pieces of Italian masters, as Mich. Angelo, Caravaggio, Tintoret, Paul Bassan Veronese, and a head by Titian, with several others of masters we neither of us know.[9]

The acquisition of such a fabulous collection by Sir Daniel Arthur indicates the wealth and taste of this extraordinary banker. The named paintings in the above quotation are worth millions today. Bagnall sold the collection to George II and the paintings now form part of the royal collection at Windsor Castle. Ironically, a collection acquired with Jacobite money helped to form the nucleus of the Hanoverian collection of paintings.

It is likely that it was Daniel Arthur who introduced Richard Cantillon to the world of banking. Arthur had already helped the Chevalier Richard Cantillon develop his banking business in Paris when he appointed him as an agent for his bank. This enabled the Chevalier to expand the international links of the bank and to increase business with the Jacobite emigres in Paris.

Unfortunately, we have no knowledge of the schooling or early career of Richard Cantillon. Part of his family, such as his elder brother Thomas, remained behind in Ireland and continued to farm their old lands as tenant farmers while Richard and his younger brother Bernard came to France.[10] In 1708 we find the earliest reference to Richard Cantillon when, following the example of his cousin the Chevalier, we find him asking for and obtaining French naturalisation.[11] Naturalisation was sought by foreigners to improve their business links in France and to protect their property, in case of death, from the *droit d'aubaine* — the right of the monarch to seize the property of deceased foreigners who died in France. We surmise that Cantillon was an adult of around twenty-one years when he made this application.

Richard Cantillon disappeared from view — that is from the notarial archives which is our main source of evidence on his early career — between 1708-14. This may have been because he travelled or alternatively he may have been learning the banking business and was not operating on his own account.

On 11 August 1714 we find Mr Richard Cantillon, living at the sign of the Cheval Noir, in the rue St Honoré in St Germain l'Auxerrois renting a carriage and two horses at a charge of 360 l.t. (£20 sterling) per month. The address given indicates that he was living with the Chevalier Richard Cantillon and the rent paid suggests that the economist was already a man of substance.[12] Just as the multi-national banker of today looks impressive with the panoply of his trade, chauffeur-driven limousines and executive jets, so also Cantillon would have been an impressive figure in his rented equipage, particularly as the contract stipulated that he would be provided with 'les chevaux d'extraordinaire' whenever visiting the court at Versailles.

Cantillon's career as a multi-national banker seems to have been concentrated on the ten year period starting with his re-appearance in Paris in 1714. Between 1714 and 1720 the bulk of his business was carried out in France, though his bank had an international clientele and a wide network of correspondents in the large financial trading centres of Europe. In the second half of 1720 he moved the main part of his operations to London and Amsterdam. His bank continued to operate in Paris to 1724 but Cantillon, subject to a retrospective tax of 2.4 million livres by the Visa in 1722, remained out of France till 1728.[13]

The period 1715-24, during which Richard Cantillon became an extremely rich and influential banker, witnessed significant changes on both the political and economic fronts. It encompassed the final days of Louis XIV, the interregnum of the Regent Philippe Duke of Orleans and the commencement of Louis XV's reign in France. It was a time of shifting political alliances with Walpole blocking a Jacobite return to the English throne through improved diplomatic relations with France, and France under the Regent's rule reluctant to embark on any grandiose foreign policy with the threat of Spain lurking close to home.

In practical terms the political disequilibria created by the deaths of Louis XIV and Anne allied with the French and British attempts to promote the new monarchical and political interests gave this part of Europe a period of respite from war and allowed for travel between Britain and France. Mobility is a key aspect of the multi-national banker's life and at a time when such bankers could not avail of modern telecommunications aids personal mobility was even more important than it is today. During this period we find Cantillon travelling frequently between the great financial centres of Amsterdam, London and Paris, a mobility that was matched by sizeable transfers of capital on his part through bank accounts in these cities.

Cantillon started his Parisian banking business in 1714/15 during a financial recession. The age of Louis XIV was drawing to an inauspicious close. The 'Sun King' died in September 1715, leaving behind a bankrupt nation with future state income mortgaged for years in advance to the financiers.

The inability of the state to honour its debts resulted in government paper selling at a massive discount. Money was extremely tight and the bankruptcy of the state had multiplier repercussions through the merchant and financial communities. Creditors who, in the past, had reasonable asset backing in the form of government securities now found this asset backing destroyed. Bankers who had made what they deemed to be good loans, on the basis of good collateral, now found their own asset backing weakening as more and more clients 'broke'. Small reserves, undercapitalisation and the collapse of government credit led to a wave of bankruptcies in the Parisian banking community in 1715.[14] Richard Cantillon, as later events indicate, learnt, or, at least had his views reinforced on the need to have good asset backing for banking loans.

Included amongst those who 'broke' was the Chevalier Richard Cantillon though this seems to have occurred more in a personal capacity than as a banker.[15] This bankruptcy, mentioned in Jacobite correspondence in 1715, took two years to surface with even then the creditors recognised 'the probity and good conduct of Mr. Cantillon' and knew that 'the difficulties in his business did not uniquely arise from losses which he made'.[16] His cousin, the economist, was to show even greater probity when he repaid the other three quarters of the Chevalier's debts outstanding after the liquidation of his assets. The economist was under no legal obligation to pay these debts, an honourable action which some commentators have distorted as further evidence of Richard Cantillon's financial duplicity.[17]

The banking problems in Paris in 1715 are mentioned in the first major financial transaction that we find Richard Cantillon handling that year. This transaction involved discounting a bill of exchange of £20,000 sterling for Lord Bolingbroke, then in hasty exile from the Whig administration:

He made arrangements in great secrecy. His first concern was to protect his wealth. He borrowed £20,000 from James Brydges, using his estates as security. These lands were then conveyed to six trustees, all political friends, who were to hold them for his wife who accepted his debts to Brydges and others.[18]

On 15 March 1715 Bolingbroke presented Cantillon with a bill of exchange, for £20,000 drawn on James Brydges, Lord Carnarvon.[19] Despite the difficulties in the Parisian banking world Cantillon succeeded in providing Bolingbroke with the required money.

Cantillon's ability to discount such a large bill of exchange and the fact that Bolingbroke addressed himself to him indicates the important role that the economist had assumed as a banker in Paris. Bolingbroke maintained his connection with Cantillon instructing Jonathan Swift, for example, to address his mail to 'M. Charlot, chez M. Cantillon, banquier, rue de l'Arbre Sec'.[20] Cantillon's friendship with Bolingbroke continued during the 1720s and they were neighbours in adjoining houses in Albemarle Street, London, when the economist's body and house were burned to ashes in 1734.[21]

Unfortunately, we have no way of determining the size of Cantillon's banking activities at this point of time. For details of his French banking career we are greatly dependent on the French notarial archives which give us glimpses of his activity but no details on his volume of turnover as unfortunately banking transactions did not require registration before a notaire.

The notarial archives do indicate that Cantillon took over his cousin the Chevalier's banking business on or before 17 February 1716, the day when he created a life pension of 3,000 livres (£184 sterling at the current exchange rate) per annum in favour of the Chevalier.[22] This was in recognition of the important 'services' which the Chevalier had rendered to Richard Cantillon, junior. *The old banking order was changing and giving way to a new one.*

The most evident indicator of this change was the establishment, through letters patent on 2 May 1716 of the General Bank (Banque Générale) under the directorship of the Scotsman, John Law. The foundation of this bank was the first step in the development of Law's Mississippi System, a system that radically transformed the French financial world between 1718 and 1720 and left memories and scars which it took decades to wipe out.

Richard Cantillon — an Irish banker in Paris

II

We must digress temporarily from Cantillon's banking activities to discuss Law's System for, as stated, it largely determined the framework in which Cantillon operated.

The System, which started slowly after the founding of the General Bank, grew remarkably quickly in 1719 and reached its apogee in the first quarter of 1720 when the Mississippi Company controlled most of the tax system, the international trading companies and the Royal Bank, which had become *de facto* a Central Bank. Its quick rise only heralded an even quicker collapse in the second half of 1720. In the first half of 1720 the System served as a model for other countries, provoking stock market booms in both London and Amsterdam. Huge sums of money were won and lost in speculation on shares, commodities and foreign exchange. By the end of 1720 Law had emerged as a major loser, lucky to escape with his life, while Cantillon, as mentioned above, was reputed to have made 20 million livres on the System.[23] Yet, despite this dramatic change in fortunes in such a short space of time Law and Cantillon had collaborated together earlier on Mississippi related deals, a fascinating collaboration representing as it did the equivalent of an eighteenth century Keynesian (Law) and monetarist (Cantillon) combining on a monetary project.

Attempting to give an overview of Law's approach to economic theory and policy is a daunting task. Anecdotal accounts of the Mississippi System abound but hard analysis of what actually happened has attracted few serious historians. Forbonnais in the eighteenth century, Levasseur in the nineteenth, and more recently Harsin, Faure, Luthy and Price have worked in a scholarly way on the System or aspects of it but sadly, as indicated above, we still lack a definitive work on the subject.[24]

We use the term system when referring to Law's financial innovations but aside from its shorthand use can we say that Law had a complete vision of the System that he had created by the spring of 1720? Like Jacob Price I do not believe that Law had a complete vision of the System when he proposed establishing the General Bank in 1715. However, the step by step development of the System had its own internal logic and was, up to the end of 1719, broadly consistent with the macroeconomic objectives Law believed economic policy needed to pursue.

Antoin E. Murphy

Price contends that:

Law was to act his hour upon the stage not as a systematic innovator but as an improvisor, changing his tactics with the circumstances.[25]

This view I would challenge to the extent that it gives the impression of Law as someone filling in patches on the economy's canvas as opportunities presented themselves but at the same time lacking 'a systematic approach'. Here I may be reading too much into Price but I find that analysis of the development of Law's System, and it was called such by contemporaries, does show a systematic approach when judged against Law's macroeconomic objectives which were:

(1) The need to increase credit through the demonetization of specie and its replacement with an augmented supply of paper credit. This expansion in credit, Law believed, would help to make more capital available for the development of underutilized resources.

(2) The need to lower interest rates to make the use of capital more attractive.[26]

If we imagine Law asking himself at each stage of the development of the System whether the particular measures in contemplation achieved either of these intermediary objectives — the ultimate objective being full employment and economic growth — then I believe we can see a systematic improvisor at work. Law himself, writing at the height of the System, was even more explicit than this describing his approach as:

Une suite d'idées qui se soutiennent les unes les autres, et qui font apercevoir de plus en plus le principe d'où elles partent.[27]

At the start of 1716 Law had certainly not a complete vision of what he would achieve five years later. He was not presented with a *carte blanche* to implement economic policy at his will. His mentor, the Regent, was in no position to give Law such powers at this time for he was still struggling with the Parlement and the court to consolidate his own power base. Little by little as Law demonstrated the success of his policies he gained the confidence of the Regent and, as the latter won victories over the Parlement and opposing court faction, Law was given more scope to advance his theories. In such an environment he was by necessity an improvisor. Opportunities had to be grasped as they presented themselves but in availing of these opportunities we can see Law systematically pursuing the macroeconomic objective of full employment, through expansionary monetary policy, that he developed as early as 1705 in *Money and trade considered*.

John Law's decision *to move from the confines of banking to debt management* has been criticized as being the major error of judgement of the Scottish economist. With hindsight vision, and here some historians of economic thought are seemingly blessed with 50/50 vision, such a view may seem correct when interpreted against the backdrop of the collapse of the System. Law, it has been contended, would have been a brilliant success if he had remained a banker and not entered the area of debt management.[28]

However, if instead of looking backwards through time we attempt to view the problem as it arose in France in 1717 we can see why Law was obliged by his own internal logic to cross the Rubicon and interest himself in debt management policy. Notwithstanding his own eulogies on the usefulness of the General Bank Law must have recognised that its role was, despite the increase in its functions, notably, the payment of taxes through the use of banknotes, extremely limited.

There were two problems: (1) the undercapitalisation of the General Bank, and (2) the massive overhang of government debt in the bond market.

Law had started off in a modest fashion. The initial capital of the General Bank was to be 6 million livres (£383,000 sterling) subscribed in 1,200 shares of 5,000 each. The effective capital base of the bank was much smaller than this due to the fact that only one quarter of the capital was to be subscribed in specie money and three quarters in *billets d'état* (a type of government security). The *billets d'état* were then at a discount of about 60% so that the effective amount of capital to be subscribed was:

Specie	1.5 million
Billets d'État (4.5 x .4)	1.8 million

3.3 million livres tournois (l.t.)

Thus at most the effective capital base of the Bank would have amounted to 3.3 million livres but even then capital was to be subscribed in four equal instalments. It is believed that only one instalment was actually paid up so that the General Bank started its operations with 825,000 livres (£52,700). Expanding the money supply to any significant extent with such a slender capital base was not possible. At the same time Law probably recognised that

55

the General Bank was having little impact on interest rates because of the huge overhang of accumulated state debt.

The banknotes issued by the General Bank were fully backed by specie and the subscription in *billets d'état* to the capital of the Bank was only 1.125 million l.t. in nominal terms. Despite the reduction in the floating debt produced by the Visa of 1716 Forbonnais estimated that there were some 250 million l.t. of *billets d'état* in circulation and 215 million l.t. of other 'papiers royaux'.[29] Additionally there were substantial long term debts in the form of annuities.

In order to lower interest rates Law needed another vehicle besides that of the General Bank and the vehicle he chose was the Company of the West (Compagnie d'Occident) which came into being in the summer of 1717. The initial proposal for the launching of this Company did not come from Law but from Le Gendre d'Arminy, brother-in-law to the great financier Crozat. The latter who owned the lease of Louisiana trade wished to surrender it, in payment of the tax levied on him through the Chamber of Justice, and so pushed, through his front man Le Gendre d'Arminy, for the creation of such a Company.[30]

By the summer of 1717 there were a variety of proposals for the creation of this type of company with a projected capitalisation varying from 2.4 million l.t. to 25 million l.t. Law, whose stature had increased *pari passu* with the growth of the General Bank, was asked for his view. He riposted with a far more grandiose proposal to establish a Company of the West with a capital of 50 million l.t. 'and perhaps more', the capital to be subscribed in *billets d'état*.

In August 1717 Law was given permission to float the Company of the West on the market. The second phase of the System was launched with as table 1 shows the issue of 200,000 shares at 500 l.t. each. As such the nominal market capitalisation was 100 million l.t. However, as the shares could only be purchased with *billets d'état*, then standing at a discount varying between 68-72 per cent, the effective market capitalisation was much smaller (30 million l.t.) and the market cost per share was between 140 and 160 l.t. — an important point when considering the growth in the market valuation of the Company's shares in later years.

As initially established the Company had two widely differing objectives: (1) the funding of part of the floating debt, and (2) the development of overseas trading. The *billets d'état* that had been subscribed for shares in the Company were transformed into 'rentes' bearing an interest rate of 4%. The income from these rentes in the first year was to form the trading capital of the Company in its efforts to colonise Louisiana. The provision of such a slim capital base to exploit the vast resources of French Louisiana indicated that the primary function of the Company was not that of developing colonial trade but of debt management, i.e. funding part of the floating debt.

To find a modern parallel is difficult but one could think of the following. The government grants a lease for offshore oil exploration to a company (mineral wealth was one of the hoped for benefits from the Louisiana concession) stipulating that the shares be subscribed for with government short term bonds, which in turn would be converted into lower yielding shares issued by the company on which a minimum dividend would be paid. As expectations improved on the company's prospects the share price of the company would rise thereby enabling it to sell more shares and fund more debt.

Law's initial problem was that the share price remained very sluggish and that the Company needed to acquire established income yielding assets to push the share price upwards. Through a series of take-overs he acquired the rights to the profitable tobacco farm lease (in return for cancelling out the 4% rentes), the lease of the Senegalese slave trade, the mint and the lease to the United Farms. These takeovers are listed in table 2 (p.70).

Through internal re-organisation of these companies he hoped to improve their profitability and on the basis of expected higher profits to raise the declared dividends on the shares. With guaranteed income sources such as those coming from the tobacco farm and united tax farms, investors were attracted to the shares of the Company particularly as Law kept revising his projected estimates of the profitability of the recently acquired companies.

Law applied a variety of new techniques in the marketing of his Company's shares to increase their public appeal. The shares were issued as bearer securities (thereby providing anonymity of ownership — an important consideration after the shock of the retrospective taxation carried out under the 1716 Visa), they were paid for by instalment (this permitted wide public participation in the share issues), and at a later stage low interest loans, to purchase shares were provided by the Royal Bank (formerly the General Bank). To increase further public interest Law introduced for a short period option trading in the Company's shares.

By the successive pyramiding of share issues on a rising share market (see table 1), Law succeeded in centralising and transforming the bulk of the French national debt by the spring of 1720. This accomplished he accentuated phase three of his policy, the demo-netization of specie and its replacement with a system of paper credit. This policy was carried through by legal enactments limiting the use of specie and by a planned series of devaluations of specie relative to banknotes and the Company's shares. These devaluations induced many holders of specie to move out of metallic money and into banknotes. With the national debt transformed into Company's shares and banknotes circulating freely it was then less risky to attempt a series of forced devaluations of specie.

The announced staggered devaluations of gold and silver coins had some success in bringing specie into the Royal Bank but by this stage Law had committed a number of cardinal errors which combined to destroy the System. These were: (1) the merger of the Royal Bank with what was then known popularly as the Mississippi Company; (2) the guarantee of a floor price of 9,000 l.t. for the Company's shares, and (3) the use of the Royal Bank's note issue to maintain this artificially high share price. *Law discovered that he could not control the interest rate and the money supply simultaneously and in attempting to keep the share price at 9,000 l.t. (a price that yielded an interest rate of 2%) he had to abandon control of the money supply.*

This brief overview of Law's System attempted to show that it involved a mixture of monetary, debt management and exchange rate policies which were combined together by Law during a frenetic eighteen months period from January 1719 to June 1720.

III

During the evolution of the System Richard Cantillon assumed in turn the role of trader-cum-coloniser, share purchaser, share seller and foreign exchange dealer. These roles saw him initially as a business colleague of Law and later an opponent of the System.

The first business arrangement between Cantillon and Law took place on 19 November 1718, at a time when Law's Company of the West was still struggling for public recognition with the shares of the Company quoted at prices considerably below their issue price.[31] Cantillon evidently recognised the growing influence of Law and entered into an agreement to form a company with the objective of establishing a settlement in French Louisiana. The company set up with a capital of 76,500 l.t. had a third partner, Joseph Edward Gage, a remarkable individual who was later to become, along with his common law wife Lady Mary Herbert, the *bête noire* of Cantillon in the 1720s and 1730s.

Up to now it was believed that Law's individual colonizing efforts started at a later date.[32] However, the notarial archives indicate this earlier attempt with Cantillon and Gage, though Law's role seems to have been that of a sleeping partner. However, he had a key role to play in allocating tracts of land in French Louisiana, and fifteen days after the decision to set up the Cantillon/Gage/Law company Richard Cantillon was granted a concession of land in French Louisiana.[33] As managing director of the Company of the West, Law could hand out concessions of land in Louisiana to friends but he may have deemed it politic not to be seen at the very start to be taking a large concession on his own account. Better to test the market first. Cantillon could equip an expedition, send it to Louisiana and report back to him on the logistics and finance involved in such a mission.

Cantillon went to work immediately and by 21 March 1719 he had equipped an expedition ready to sail from La Rochelle. The expedition was headed by Cantillon's younger brother Bernard and numbered thirty-seven men and three women. While the number listed on the ship's papers appears somewhat small compared to some of the more ambitious expeditions that were to follow in 1720, one can see the hand of Cantillon at work when consulting the passenger list.[34] The expedition was a well-balanced one, including as it did two carpenters and a joiner, a miller and two bakers, two coopers, two tailors, a miner and refiner, a farrier, a cartwright, a wig-maker, a clerk, four labourers and a servant. One can see Cantillon diligently selecting those trades that he considered important for the establishment of a settlement in Louisiana and for vital activities such as carpentry and breadmaking ensuring that there was a replacement in the eventuality of one of these key tradesmen dying during the trip.

The occupations of a number of people on this expedition is not listed. Some of these people were Irish, Robert Cook, Denis Soulboone (Sullivan), William Leyne, Thomas Hussey and Jeanne Broone (Browne). There were four Englishmen on the expedition, two of which, Jonathan Darby and John Darling, seem to have been Bernard Cantillon's principal assistants.[35]

It is probable that Richard Cantillon in helping to prepare this expedition, which seems to have been far better manned and equipped than any of the groups sent to Louisiana in 1718, gained some first hand knowledge of wage determination in the labour market, a knowledge he was later to show in book one of the *Essai*.

Cantillon's willingness to finance, in part, such an expedition also gives us an insight into his comments on the role of the entrepreneur, the risk taker committing himself to purchasing factors of production at a known price in order to market their output at an unknown but hopefully higher price.[36] This was risk-taking on a substantial basis — equipping a large force of men and sending them thousands of miles away from France to an area the possibilities of which were largely unknown. It may be noted that Cantillon sent a miner and refiner on this expedition with the hope that mineral wealth might be discovered.

Bernard Cantillon surmounted considerable problems in establishing a settlement about two hundred and sixty kilometres due north of New Orleans. Notwithstanding the fact that this settlement was not viable in the long run, Bernard Cantillon returning to France in 1723, his expedition to North America was probably not in vain. He was in a position to provide expert commentary on what was happening in the colony to his brother and so enable the economist to discount the glowing reports on Louisiana that were circulating in Paris during the spring of 1720. The Jesuit traveller Fr Charlevoix pointed out some years later that the New Orleans he visited bore little resemblance to that described in the *Mercure de France* in early 1720. Instead of the eight hundred fine houses and five parishes that comprised the New Orleans described by the *Mercure,* Fr Charlevoix found on his arrival in 1722 only 'one hundred randomly situated huts, a large wooden store and two or three houses unworthy of any French village'.[37]

While Richard and Bernard Cantillons' efforts at colonization were not rewarded with great success Richard, a business colleague with Law from the early days of the System, was in a key position to benefit from the massive rise in share prices that took place in 1719. Cantillon was estimated as having made 20 million l.t. out of the System but an examination of his accounts for 1720 indicate that at most his profits in Paris for that year were 6.5 million l.t. The implication of this is that if one accepts the Visa estimate of Cantillon's profits he made a considerable part of them in 1719. However, he seemed to have reservation on the viability of the System and he left France for Italy leaving his banking business under the management of another Irish banker, Edmund Loftus, in the summer of 1719.

Richard Cantillon — an Irish banker in Paris

This business relationship did not last very long as Cantillon indicated in a letter to another banker Martin Harrold in March 1720:

At my going to Italy I wrote to you in favour of Messrs. Loftus and Company to whom I recommended all my affairs and correspondence. And I may say I left my house in as good credit and business as any house. But at my return, having had some reason to repent the great confidence I reposed in Mr. Loftus, the chief of the Company, I have in order to support the business engaged Mr. Hughes of London to come over to take upon him the management of my affairs and to engage in partnership with my nephew under the name of Cantillon and Hughes — I gave in my procuration to look after my interest in the commandite of Loftus and Company — whereof the whole capital belongs to me and two thirds of the profit for the time the said company has to run. I shall be glad when you have balanced the accounts now depending with the said Loftus and Company. You run on for the future with the said Cantillon and Hughes who will be strongly supported in their business. I shall be obliged for the sake of my nephew and my name to put the house upon a good footing. Mr. Loftus after settling the accounts depending is to go out of the house and I am persuaded you will be served for the future with punctuality and satisfaction. The following signing of Cantillon and Hughes alone will govern you in the affairs of this house.[38]

This letter illustrates that there was a major rift between Edmund Loftus and Richard Cantillon. A further indicator of the nature of the difficulties that arose may be inferred from the more detailed contractual relationship governing the 'commandite' between the economist, John Hughes and his nephew. Under the contract establishing the 'commandite' John Hughes was subject to considerable surveillance by his 'sleeping partner' Richard Cantillon, While the Cantillon/Loftus contract did not go into specific detail on the running of the company we find under the new contract that Richard Cantillon had the right to hire and fire employees, that the account books of the company were to be drawn up daily and be ready for examination by Richard Cantillon at any time, that the economist had a right to close down the company at any stage and that John Hughes was constrained from working for his own private account.[39] It was perhaps this last issue which caused difficulties between Loftus and Cantillon.

Savary's *Dictionnaire universel de commerce* informs us that the basis of the 'commandite' arrangement was that one partner subscribed capital and the other his labour.[40] This type of partnership derived its name from the fact that the person who subscribed capital is 'always the boss and in a position, so to speak, to command and to lay down the law relative to his partner'.[41] The benefit of this arrangement was that it enabled capital and labour to be meshed together with the provider of capital usually not wishing to run the day-to-day operations of the partnership while his associate, furnishing little or no capital, devoted himself full time to the enterprise. Additionally, the liability of the 'commandite' was limited to the share capital that he subscribed.

Cantillon raised the share capital for the new partnership to 50,000 l.t. stipulating that the partnership would operate for twenty years and that he would be entitled to two-thirds of the profits and John Hughes to one-third.[42] Rather surprisingly a third person, Richard Cantillon junior, the nephew of the economist, then aged four, was included in the business. This inclusion of the nephew was later construed by Cantillon's commentators as an action aimed at duping clients of the bank in that the economist was using his nephew's name to give the impression that it was he (the economist) who was running the business whereas in reality he was limiting his involvement to a capital investment of 50,000 l.t.[43] This, I feel, is attaching too much credence to the accounts of Cantillon's adversaries. An alternative and more plausible explanation was that the nephew was included in the partnership arrangement so that he would be the beneficiary of his uncle's investment in the case of the economist dying.

Having established this new partnership Cantillon involved the bank in a number of large loans between March and May. These loans are summarised in table 3. It indicates that in the two months between 12 March and 11 May Cantillon's bank lent £53,032 sterling to a group comprising Joseph Gage, Lady Mary Herbert, Lord Montgomery, a brother of Lady Mary, and two Irish bankers John and Remy Carol. In each case collateral in the form of Mississippi shares was given for the loans.

The size of the loans and collateral offered show that Joseph Gage and Lady Mary Herbert were substantial Mississippians riding on the crest of the 'bull' market in these shares. Gage and Herbert were sufficiently well known to be satirized by Alexander Pope in the *Epistle to Bathurst*, written in 1731 and published in 1733:

> The Crown of Poland, venal twice an age,
> To just three millions stinted modest Gage.
> But nobler scenes Maria's dreams unfold,
> Hereditary Realms, and world of Gold.
> Congenial souls! whose life one Av'rice joins,
> And one fate buries in th' Asturian Mines.[44]

Richard Cantillon — an Irish banker in Paris

The first couplet refers to Joseph Gage's supposed attempt to purchase the crown of Poland from the venal Polish nobility for three million livres. On being turned down Gage then attempted to purchase the island of Sardinia. Lady Mary Herbert (Maria) was even more ambitious as Horace Walpole indicated by the following annotation to his copy of Pope's *Epistle:*

Lady Mary Herbert, sister of the last Marquis of Powis, had made a prodigious fortune in the Mississippi, and refused the Duke of Bouillon, being determined to marry nobody but a Sovereign Prince; but refusing to realise, lost the whole, and met Gage in the Asturian mines.[45]

Mentioned as a possible wife for the Jacobite Pretender, James III, Lady Mary Herbert never realised her lofty ambitions and as Horace Walpole pointed out spent a considerable time after the Mississippi debacle in Spain mining for precious metals, an activity then shared with the penniless Joseph Gage.

It is important to ask why prominent Mississippians, the sobriquet of heavy traders in shares in the Rue Quinquempoix, wanted to borrow such large amounts from Cantillon. Why did they not sell some of their shares or at least borrow from the Royal Bank? An account by one of Cantillon's lawyers explains the reason for this borrowing:

At or about that time many persons became adventurers in the public funds in France which made the price of those funds and particularly French India actions rise very considerably and a general opinion prevailed in France that the price of such actions would rise considerably more, and several arrets having been issued in France for the reduction of the current specie there, which was then very high. The general opinion there also was that French money would in a few months be worth much more in sterling money than it was then worth and that consequently the course of exchange betwixt London and Paris which was then about 13^d sterling for a French crown would be in December following at 50^d sterling. Joseph Edward Gage, Lady Mary Herbert and Lord Montgomery were in the years 1720 at Paris and being possessed of a great quantity of French East India actions and being desirous to deal in the stocks in England and wanting ready money, but not being willing to make sale of their said India actions, they applied to Cantillon Senior and the partnership of Cantillon and Hughes for the loan of several great sums of money to be paid them in sterling money in England in a short space of time, upon a security of their bills of exchange and notes payable at a distant day for the several sums which the parties should agree upon to settle the exchange at and on their making a deposit of French India actions for the better securing the payment thereof, which Cantillon Senior and the partnership of Cantillon and Hughes agreed to.[46]

The demand for these loans was sparked off by the order of 11 March 1720 stipulating a progressive devaluation of specie in France.[47] Gage and Lady Mary Herbert, large scale beneficiaries of Law's System, and probably members of his inner coterie, believed that John Law, then Controller General of Finances, would be successful in carrying out this new policy. The prospect of such a success, the staggered devaluation of specie in France, opened up the possibility of potential foreign exchange gains.

Unwilling to sell their shares they borrowed foreign exchange using the shares as collateral, Gage and Herbert borrowing in sterling and the Carol brothers in Dutch florins. They then remitted their foreign borrowings to France in the naive belief that as the French crown fell relative to banknotes they would have to repay less French crowns on the maturity of their loans. Cantillon disagreed with their expectations on both the price of Mississippi shares, which they were unwilling to sell believing that they would rise higher, and on the expected exchange rate on the maturity of the loans.

It is quite clear from reading Cantillon's letters to John Hughes and others that he believed the System would collapse in the second half of 1720.[48] Accordingly, given his first hand experience of the banking problems encountered between 1714-17, he took steps to protect his bank. The collateral backing of Mississippi shares for the bank's loans was very much dependent on the success of Law's policies, a success which Cantillon believed in no longer. The merger of the Royal Bank into the Mississippi Company, the attempts to induce the public to substitute banknotes for specie and the use of the Bank's printing presses to force the price of shares upwards (thereby forcing the rate of interest down to 2 per cent) were judged with an increasingly jaundiced eye by Cantillon. He was later to summarise this scepticism on his part in the final lines of the *Essai:*

It is certain that a Bank in agreement with a Minister is capable, when the operation is carried out discreetly, of raising and maintaining the price of public stock and of lowering the rate of interest in the state, according to Ministerial wishes, and by this to free the State of its debts. But these refinements, which provide the means to make large fortunes, are rarely administered for the exclusive benefit of the state, *more often than not corrupting those involved in them.* The excess banknotes which are issued and circulated on these occasions do not disturb circulation as they are not used for everyday expenditure serving instead for the purchase and sale of stock and not being cashed in for coin. But if through fear or some unforeseen accident their holders look for coin from the Bank, the bubble would burst and these operations would be seen to be dangerous.[49]

This was not just a retrospective view. Cantillon sold a large quantity of Mississippi stock in the spring of 1720, remitting these funds to London and Amsterdam. He recognised that manipulations of the domestic exchange rate, through devaluations and revaluations, could only have a short term effect. He is quite explicit on this point in many parts of the *Essai:*

All people are full of false prejudice and false ideas as to the nominal value of their coinage. We have shewn in the Chapter of Exchanges that the invariable rule of them is the price and fineness of the current coins of different countries, marc for marc and ounce for ounce. If a raising or lowering of the nominal value changes this rule for a time in France it is only during a crisis and difficulty in trade. A return is always made little by little to intrinsic value, to which prices are necessarily brought both in the market and in the foreign exchanges.[50]

Having successfully remitted the bulk of his funds to Amsterdam and London by the summer of 1720 Cantillon then diverted his attention to the speculative boom in Holland and to a lesser extent the South Sea Bubble in London. Cantillon's success on the European stock exchanges was considerable as is evidenced in a letter from the commercial representative at the British Embassy in Paris, Pulteney, to the British Government. This letter also shows that Law was making strenuous efforts to 'encourage' his former business colleague back to Paris:

Monsieur Cantillion who was a banker here and got considerably by the Mississippi, which he improved in the South Sea, and in the stocks in Holland, where he now is, has been pressed by Mr. Law to return and settle here, with great offers of preferment. He has hitherto declined it, upon which it has been signified to him, that if he does not comply with these offers they will not pay some bills to the value of £20,000 sterling which he had drawn for copper he bought in Holland by commission for the company and has sent here, but that this sum shall be reckoned as a tax on him for his gains in the Mississippi.
It is thought that the bank bills which still remain in the public will on some pretence or other be called in to the bank, and that this will be done to oblige the anciens actionnaires to purchase in money the actions they are to deposit or to purchase bills for money at par. . . .

Mr. Law lies sometimes at his own house and sometimes at the Palais Royal. When he removes it is not in his own equipage and it is observed that the swiss guards are dispersed about. . . .[51]

Pulteney's letter indicates that Cantillon showed great ability in anticipating the peaks in stock market prices in three European countries in 1720, moving into and out of shares first in Paris, then in London and finally in Amsterdam.[52] This expertise was apparently recognised by Law who at the time Pulteney's letter was written, 7 November 1720, was in desperate need of a financial 'stroke' to save the System. The growing crowds of disenchanted Mississippians were baying for his blood and as Pulteney shows Law had to conceal his movements from this Parisian mob.

It is believed that Law wished to make use of Cantillon's expertise in financial matters to save the System. The fact that Law went to such lengths, with a mixture of promises and threats, shows the stature that Cantillon had in his eyes as a financial manipulator. Interpreted in this light this view tends to corroborate Grimm's account that Cantillon had earlier intervened at a critical juncture in the System's history to support the Mississippi shares in the market.[53]

But the Irishman was no longer prepared to attempt a second lifeboat operation for the System. Indeed he had already taken steps to counter Law's punitive threat by impounding the copper which he had bought, on William Law's instructions, in Amsterdam.

Cantillon's financial ability was known to others beside Law, for in December 1720 he was sounded out by Lady Mary Herbert, with whom he was still on letter writing terms, as to whether he would be willing to become a director of the Mississippi Company:

As to what your Ladyship desires to know viz. whether it would be agreeable to me to be made a director of the Company there I can only say that I don't understand it and that considering the French would be apt to be jealous of any foreigner after Mr. Law's proceedings I don't desire to be concerned amongst them. There is an air of freedom and property in this island that would tempt me very much to stay here for good if I could enjoy lands in it but even as it is I am not in haste to go back.[54]

Cantillon declined the invitation and due to the wealth tax of the 1721 Visa did not return to France till 1727. Law left France in haste, under an assumed name, just before Christmas 1720. He attempted to revive the Regent's interest in his financial plans but the latter's death in 1723 destroyed his ambitions to resurrect the

Richard Cantillon — an Irish banker in Paris

System in a new guise. John Law died in Venice in 1729 not, as historians would have us believe, in poor circumstances but a wealthy man, owner of a very substantial collection of old masters which included works by Tintoretto, Raphael, David, Murillo, Rubens, Poussin, Vandyke, etc.[55] Law despite his protestations that he was broken by the System must have been able to salt part of the gains he made out of France in the form of paintings, The traditional image of Law dying impecunious in Venice, of a man broken by his own efforts to improve society, of a financial manipulator who placed the welfare of society before his own private interest, must be re-considered in the light of his hitherto unrevealed wealth at the time of his death.[56]

SUMMARY

John Law was very much an eighteenth-century Keynesian, though surprisingly Keynes never mentioned him in the *General Theory*. Even when writing the preface to the French edition of the *General Theory* Keynes declared Montesquieu to be the great eighteenth-century French economist, a declaration showing the superficiality of Keynes's knowledge of eighteenth-century economic thought. Law was a man very much ahead of his time who clearly identified the resource cost implications of a metallic money system, resource costs in terms of the use of factors of production to mine gold and silver only to re-inter it at a later stage in the vaults of banks, resource costs in terms of the shortage of specie to oil the wheels of trade, resource costs in terms of the high interest rate which deterred investment, the high interest rate caused by the ease with which specie could be hoarded.

Law's System which aimed to demonetize specie, to make credit more easily available and to lower the rate of interest was very modern in its conception. However, the System failed.

The *Essai sur la nature du commerce en général* was written, in part, to explain the failure of the System. Cantillon had been involved with Law's System from its inception and it continued to occupy his attention long after its collapse due to the lawsuits arising out of his Mississippi dealings. Cantillon needed to explain why the System failed and at the same time to justify his own particular behaviour during it. A propos the litigation he was involved in one finds some close parallels between his chapter on the rate of interest and on foreign exchange and the defence brief his lawyer, Maître

Cochin, presented against the Carol brothers, where the accusation of Cantillon lending funds across the foreign exchanges at usurious rates of interest was countered.[57]

Cantillon never explicitly mentions Law or the failures of the System in the *Essai*. At the same time it reads like a scholarly refutation of the dangers of overexpanding the money supply, manipulating the exchange rate and attempting to control the rate of interest.[58] Cantillon by not being overtly specific in his indictment of Law's System left us with a work that goes beyond the problems of the eighteenth century. He was no dogmatist pushing a hard line that increases in the money supply always produced proportionate increases in prices. He introduced velocity of circulation as an important variable on the left hand side of the equation of exchange. He recognised that increases in the money supply could have positive short term benefits on employment and output.[59]

He distinguished between traded and non-traded goods and recognised that in an open economy with a mixture of traded and non-traded goods increases in the money supply would have different effects on the prices of these goods, as well as balance of payments implications. He identified the need for Central Bank open market operations but at the same time he was fearful about excessive intervention by the government in macroeconomic policy. Quite simply Cantillon did not trust the politicians; the last lines of the *Essai*, already quoted, clearly show this. Allow politicians to expand the money supply and they end up overexpanding it. They become prisoners of the system. Recent events indicate that this message is still of relevance in the twentieth century.

TABLE 1: Share issues by the Mississippi Company

Date		Shares issued	Nominal price	Cost	Nominal value	Terms
June & Sept 1717	Mères	200,000	500	140-160	100 million	Shares bought with *billets d'Etat*
June 1719	Filles	50,000	500	550	25 million	Paid in 20 instalments. Had to have 4 old shares for 1 new.
July 1719	Petites Filles	50,000	500	1,000	50 million	Paid in 20 instalments of 50. 4 Mères & 1 Filles for 1 new.
26 September 1719		100,000	500	5,000	50 million	Paid in 10 instalments of 500.
28 September 1719		100,000	500	5,000	50 million	As above. Meant to be reserved for office holders etc.
2 October 1719		100,000	500	5,000	50 million	As above.
4 October 1719		24,000				
		624,000				

On 29 November 1719 Dutot calculated the market value of the 624,000 shares of the Mississippi Company at 4,781,750,000 livres tournois (average price per share of 7,663 l.t.).

TABLE 2: The development of Law's System

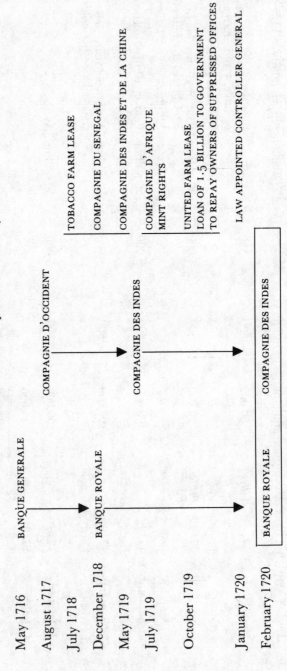

TABLE 3: Loans by Cantillon and Hughes to Joseph Gage, the Carol brothers and the Powis family in 1720

Date	Borrowers	Loan	Capital to be paid and length of loan	Collateral	Supplementary Collateral
12 March	Joseph Gage[1]	£16,433	£21,389 (one loan for 12 months two loans for 6 months)	140 shares	180 shares (June 9)
20 March	Jean & Remy Carol	35,000 fl.	41,000 fl. (8 months)	20 shares	20 shares (June 12)
11 April	Lady Mary Herbert	£15,333	£23,850 (8 months)	93 shares	
12 April	Lord Montgomery	£5,000	£7,777 (8 months)	40 shares	
11 May	Lady Mary Herbert	£13,336	£20,000 (£10,000 due in December & the same in January)	80 shares	

[1]Gage drew two bills on (1) Martin Darcy for £14,259.14.10 and (2) the Marquis of Powis for £7,129.12.5. Gage, according to Thomas Molagne (AN, MC LXXXII11/346), made his first borrowing on 12 March for £6,180 sterling. He made further borrowings on 12 and 18 March.

Antoin E. Murphy

Notes

1. The background to the publication of Cantillon's *Essai sur la nature du commerce en général* (1755) is discussed in Antoin Murphy *'Le Développement des idées economiques en France 1754-58'*, *Revue d'Histoire Moderne et Contemporaine* (forthcoming). All references to the *Essai* are taken from Henry Higgs (ed.) *Essai sur la nature du commerce en général* (London, 1931).

2. Sir John Hicks, *Critical essays in monetary theory* (Oxford, 1967), p. 156.

3. Antoin Murphy, 'Richard Cantillon: banker and economist', *Journal of Libertarian Studies* (forthcoming).

4. Joseph Hone, 'Richard Cantillon, economist — biographical note' in *Economic Journal* 54 (April 1944).

5. W. A. Shaw, *The knights of England*, Vol. 2 (London, 1906).

6. H. M. C. *Finch* 11 (1922), p. 482. My translation from the French text.

7. *Some thoughts on the Bill depending before the House of Lords for prohibiting the exportation of the woollen manufactures of Ireland to foreign parts* (London, 1698), p. 5. See L. M. Cullen, 'The exchange business of the Irish banks in the eighteenth century' in *Economica,* (November, 1958), p. 332.

8. Paris, Archives Nationales, Minutier Central (henceforth AN, MC), LXVI-364, 23 Septembre, 1717. Inventaire après décès de Richard Cantillon.

9. H. M. C. Egmont 111, (1923). p. 344.

10. Antoin Murphy, 'Richard Cantillon, banker and economist', *op.cit.*

11. Paris, Archives Nationales, O¹ 52, Fol. 202. 'Naturalité pour Richard Cantillon natif de Ballironane dans le Comté de Kerry en Irlande. A Versailles au mois d'Avril 1708.'

12. AN, MC 1-258. Bail de Carosse à Richard Cantillon, Aoust 11, 1714.

13. Du Hautchamp, *Histoire générale et particulière du Visa* (La Haye, 1743), Vol. 2, p. 170.

14. For an account of some of these bankruptcies at this time see Herbert Luthy, *La Banque protestante en France* (Paris, 1959), Vol. 1.

15. H. M. C. Stuart 111, (1907) p. 406. A letter from Arbuthnot dated 18 July 1715, mentions 'Mr. Chantillon's breaking spoils the King's measures'.

16. AN, MC LXVI-362, 13 Avril 1717. On this point see Guy Antonetti, 'Autour de Cantillon' (*Mémoires de la Société pour l'Histoire du Droit*, Dijon), p. 9.

17. See for example, Anita Fage 'La Vie et l'oeuvre de Richard Cantillon', in *Richard Cantillon Essai sur la nature du commerce en général,* (INED, Paris 1958) p. xxvi. See also Henry Higgs, 'Richard Cantillon', *Economic Journal,* Vol. 1 (1891), pp 284-285.

18. H. T. Dickinson, *Bolingbroke* (London, 1970).

19. AN, MC LXVI-368, Déclaration par Richard Cantillon, 21 Mars 1719.

20. Harold Williams (ed.), *The correspondence of Jonathan Swift,* (Oxford, 1963), Bolingbroke to Swift, October 23, 1716: volume 2, p. 217.

21. Abbé Prévost, *Le Pour et contre,* Nombre XLVIII, Vol. 4 (1734), pp 49-55. Prévost describes Bolingbroke, suspicious about the circumstances of the murder, sifting through the ruins of Cantillon's house.

22. AN, MC, LXVI-358, 17 Février, 1716.

23. The traditional view accepted by biographers of Law such as H. Montgomery Hyde, *John Law* (London, 1969) and Edgar Faure *La Banqueroute de Law* (Gallimard, Paris, 1977) is that Law was left penniless by the System. This view is very much open to question as will be shown in note 56 below.

24. Francois Veron de Forbonnais, *Recherches et considérations sur les finances de France depuis 1595 jusqu'en 1721* (1758); Emile Levasseur *Recherches historiques sur le Système de Law* (1854, reprinted Burt Franklin, New York, 1970); Paul Harsin, *Crédit public et Banque d'Etat en*

72

Richard Cantillon — an Irish banker in Paris

France du XVIe au XVIIIe Siècle (Paris, 1933); Marcel Giraud, *Histoire de la Louisiane Francaise*, vol. III, L'Epoque de John Law (Paris, 1966); J. M. Price, *France and the Chesapeake* (Univ. of Michigan, 1973); Edgar Faure, *op.cit.*; Herbert Luthy, *op.cit.*

25. J. M. Price, *op.cit.*, p. 198.

26. John Law, *Oeuvres complètes*, ed. Paul Harsin, (Paris, 1934, reprint 1980).

27. John Law, *Oeuvres, op.cit.*, vol. 3, pp 98-99. This letter appeared in the *Mercure de France* in February 1720.

28. See, for example, Courcelle-Seneuil's article on John Law in L. Say and J. Chailley's *Nouveau dictionnaire d'economie politique* (Paris, 1892), Vol. 2, p. 128.

29. Forbonnais, *op.cit.*

30. Price, *op.cit.*, pp 205-220.

31. Paris, AN, MC LXVI-370, 31 Juillet 1719 and 23 Aoust 1719. Procuration Richard Cantillon à Edmund Loftus.

32. Marcel Giraud, *op.cit.*, vol. 3, p. 181, notes that it was in July 1719 that Law was granted a large concession in Louisiana. Our evidence suggests that Law was involved with Cantillon in a Louisiana concession eight months earlier on 19 November 1718. For Law's views on colonisation see *Oeuvres*, vol. III, p. 263.

33. Giraud, *op.cit.*, p. 177. Giraud gives the date of the granting of Cantillon's concession as 5 December, 1718.

34. Paris, Archives Nationales, F⁵B57, 'Passagers embarqués en France-La Rochelle, 1718-1828'; see also Paris, Archives Coloniales, G¹ 464, folio 9.

35. *Ibid.*

36. *Essai*, p. 51. For a more extended commentary on Cantillon's view of the entrepreneur see Robert Herbert and Albert N. Link, *The entrepreneur* (New York, 1982), pp 14-22.

37. Pierre de Charlevoix, *Journal historique d'un voyage fair par ordre du roi dans l'Amerique septentrionale* (Paris, 1744), Vol. 6, pp 192-193.

38. Aberystwyth, National Library of Wales, Powis Castle Correspondence, 11, 194.

39. Paris, AN, MC LXVI, 375. 19 Avril 1720, Procuration Richard Cantillon à Jean Hughes. Also Stafford, County Record Office, D 641/2/C/3/8 Mr. Lake's Case.

40. Savary, *Dictionnaire universel de commerce* (Paris 1723), Vol. 2, pp 1550-1551.

41. *Ibid.*

42. *Loc.cit.*, AN, MC LXVI, 375.

43. Anita Fage in *Essai* (INED, Paris, 1952), *op.cit.*, pp xxvi-xxvii.

44. Alexander Pope, 'Epistle to Allen, Lord Bathurst', in Alexander Pope, *Epistles to several persons*, ed. F. W. Bateson (London, 1951), pp 100-101.

45. *Ibid*, note on p. 101.

46. Stafford, County Record Office D 641/2/C/3/8. Mr. Lake's Case. Bibye Lake acted as the English solicitor to Cantillon's family.

47. See Faure, *op.cit.*, pp. 357-359.

48. See letters quoted by Henry Higgs in 'Richard Cantillon', *Economic Journal*, Vol. 1 (1891), pp 262-291.

49. *Essai*, p. 322. I have translated this into English as I found Higgs' translation inadequate.

50. *Essai*, p. 299.

51. London, P.R.O., S.P. 78/166. Letter from Daniel Pulteney (Commissioner and Representative on Colonies and Trade with France) in Paris to James Craggs (Principal Secretary of State at the Southern Department), 7 November 1720.

52. Richard Hyse, 'Richard Cantillon, financier to Amsterdam, July to November 1720', *Economic Journal*, December 1971.

53. Grimm, *Corréspondance littéraire, philosophique et critique par Grimm, Diderot, Raynal* (Paris, 1878). Letter written by Grimm on 1 August 1755.

54. Aberystwyth, National Library of Wales, Powis Castle Correspondence 10,726. Copy of letter from Richard Cantillon to Lady Mary Herbert, 9 January 1721.

55. Th. P. M. Huijs, *Inventaire des archives de John Law et de William Law 1715-1734* (Maestricht, 1978), p. 111. This inventory indicates that on 6 August 1729 there were eighty-one cases containing pictures and works of art in Venice belonging to Katherine Knollys, widow of John Law.

56. H. Montgomery Hyde, *op.cit.*, made the following observation: 'All the property the once rich and famous Controller-General left at his death was several thousand livres which he had won at the tables, a few pictures, he had bought with his winnings . . .' (p. 210).

57. Paris, Bibliothèque Nationale, Fol. Factum 2,740. *Memoire pour Richard Cantillon contre Jean et Remi Carol*, pp 8-9, can be compared with pp 253-256 of the *Essai*.

58. Cantillon's work on monetary theory and his implied criticism of Law's System is to be found in books 2 and 3 of the *Essai*. Book 1 is more concerned with value theory, location theory and population theory. Interestingly references to the missing Supplement only occur in Book 1, raising the possibility that there was a significant time gap between the writing of Book 1 and Books 2 and 3.

59. Antoin Murphy, 'Richard Cantillon: banker and economist', *op.cit.*

0440
8410
Ireland
0322
Malthus, Thomas R.

75-95

Malthus and the pre-famine economy

by Cormac Ó Gráda

> Ireland's case affords so striking an illustration of the doctrines of which Mr. Malthus has advanced in the late *Essay on Population,* that we are surprised he did not enter into it more in detail.
>
> Anon. (T. R. Malthus, *Edinburgh Review,* 1808)

> The destiny of Ireland in the early nineteenth century was very largely moulded by the ideas of two great economists, Adam Smith and Malthus, and of the two the latter was probably the more influential.
>
> George O'Brien (*The Economic History of Ireland from the Union to the famine,* 1921)

There is a slightly implausible scene towards the end of Thomas Flanagan's *Year of the French* where one of the main characters, a Mayo clergyman, is spending Christmas 1798 with a brother in Derbyshire. One evening, the local vicar lends him the recently-published *Essay on the principle of population.* Being a short work, it did not take him long to read, but 'clear and cold as ice water, it clarified and chilled the brain'. Many since have shared the Rev. Mr Broome's reaction to Malthus's 'unimpassioned calm', in dooming the Irish 'to an endless sequence of spawning and starving, spawning and starving'.[1] But Malthus has had vigorous and steady support too over the years, from economists, historians, and policy makers. By coincidence, Malthusian exegesis is in great vogue at present, and Ireland's prominent role in it is a good reason for this paper.

In the course of his recent television serial on the history of economics, John Kenneth Galbraith termed the Great Irish Famine a 'triumphant validation' of the ideas of Malthus. 'No one could doubt', claimed Galbraith, 'the tendency of the Irish population (to) increas(e) geometrically. Within a mere sixty years . . . it first doubled and then very nearly doubled again . . .' The agricultural revolution based on potato cultivation could not keep food supply in line, and the blight of 1845-7, 'a Malthusian climax', merely confirmed food supply's loss in its race against population. William

The author thanks his colleagues Des Norton, John Sheehan, Moore McDowell, Brendan Walsh and Fergus D'Arcy, and David Dickson of T.C.D. for their comments and advice.

Cormac Ó Gráda

Petersen's *Malthus,* published in 1979, also points to Ireland as 'a "Malthusian" country', and devotes several pages to explaining 'how a better food supply helped build up a greater population pressure'. More recently still, David Grigg's historical monograph on population and land supply devotes a long chapter to Ireland under the heading, 'Malthus justified'.[2] The evidence for this chain of reasoning — from potatoes to overpopulation, from overpopulation to Great Famine — seems so compelling that the 'Malthusian' view has come to dominate historical analysis of the Irish economy in the nineteenth century. The doyen of Irish economic historians, Louis Cullen, quotes approvingly an American lady who visited Ireland in 1844: 'there must needs be an explosion of some kind or another'.[3] In the very wake of the Famine, land agent Steuart Trench sold the same line to his friend, economist Nassau Senior:[4]

It was an awful remedy. The country wore a delusive appearance of prosperity. Capital had been accumulating — rents had risen, and were well paid . . . the value of property was increasing; but all this time the population was increasing more rapidly than the capital that was to maintain and employ it. . . . Such were its numbers that it seemed irrevocably doomed to the potato. . . . Nothing but the successive failures of the potato, its failure season after season, could have produced the emigration which will, I trust, give us room to become civilized.

In this now standard view, the Famine was no more than a classic positive check — 'the ultimate Malthusian catastrophe'[5] — to an economy that had run completely out of control. Inevitable and even necessary, the Famine cruelly 'dramatized the risks of improvident marriage'.[6] The cure was in proportion to the remedy: so effective was it that Irish caution about getting married became legendary. The model of population growth suggested by this approach has been popularized in many places: the potato facilitated early marriage, and reduced the death rate for a time, by providing a more varied food supply. However, by 1800 or so dependence on the root had already gone too far, and society was locked in a poverty trap and a 'vortex of subdivision'.[7] Disaster threatened, because the Irish were by then too numerous to switch to less productive but safer crops, and too poor to leave the island.

The Malthusian approach was not limited to history or retrospective analysis, however. Economic views that today would be regarded as hard-line Malthusian had quite an innings in prefamine Ireland. Against all proposals for betterment, somebody was bound to raise the bogey of population. Reducing rents would 'speedily

76

land (the peasant) on the verge of famine on the fertile land'; poor relief could 'never be given without leading to most mischievous consequences'; emigration could provide only a temporary respite; and so on. During the Famine itself, the 'principle of population' created a climate of opinion which rationalized over-cautious relief, and great emphasis on the abuse of 'spongers'.[8] Few contemporary observers took a completely negative line on all policy proposals, of course, but no economist had an acceptable panacea for Ireland's admittedly serious problems either. Perhaps it is little wonder that Malthus became somewhat of a *bête noire* in popular and nationalist circles. In this paper, we will review first what 'Population Malthus' himself had to say on Ireland, and then re-examine prefamine Ireland in that light.

I.   WHAT MALTHUS HAD TO SAY

Given Ireland's pride of place in Malthusian historiography and exegesis, Malthus's own relative lack of interest in Irish affairs is quite surprising. In its quest for case studies, the first edition of the *Principles* — better known in the history of economics as the *First essay* — wanders from Pomerania to New Jersey, and from Naples to China, but totally ignores Ireland.[9] Nor is the promise held out by the title of Chapter 10, Book I, of the second edition — the so-called 'quarto edition' or *Second essay* — 'Of the preventive check in Scotland and Ireland', delivered. Ireland warrants only the following paragraph, repeated virtually unchanged in subsequent editions:[10]

The details of the population of Ireland are but little known. I shall only observe, therefore, that the extended use of potatoes has allowed a very rapid increase of it during the last century. But the cheapness of this nourishing root, and the small piece of ground which, under this kind of cultivation, will, on average years produce the food for a family, joined with ignorance and barbarism of the people, which have promoted them to follow their inclinations with no prospect than immediate bare subsistence, have encouraged marriage to such a degree, that the population is pushed much beyond the industry and present resources of the country; and the consequence naturally is, that the lower classes of people are in the most depressed and miserable state. The checks to the population are of course chiefly of the positive kind, and arise from the diseases occasioned by squalid poverty, by damp and wretched cabins, by bad and insufficient clothing, by the filth of their persons, and occasional want. To these positive checks have, of late years, been added the vice and misery of intestine commotion, of civil war, and of martial law.

These two hundred or so words come after six thousand words on the 'Checks to population in the islands of the South Sea', four thousand on 'Indostan and Tibet' and four thousand more on 'Siberia, Northern and Southern'. And apart from some passing references, that is all. Malthus's evident lack of interest in Ireland puzzles us today as much as it did Flanagan's Mr Broome. 'On other occasions', wrote a contemporary critic, 'Mr. Malthus seems quite alive in the pursuit of information; we can trace him in most countries of Europe, especially its wildest parts, examining records, consulting professors, taking every opportunity of communicating with the lower orders of people'. In the case of Ireland, however, 'it does not appear that he ever saw the country, consulted a document, or asked a simple question about so important a part of the United Kingdom'. Patricia James, who has recently rescued this quotation from oblivion, rightly sees it as 'the plain truth'.[11] In the sixth edition, written some years after Malthus's only known visit to Ireland in July 1817, the insensitive reference to 'barbarism' was replaced by 'depressed state' and, further down the paragraph, 'depressed' by 'impoverished'. In addition, the bare results of the 1821 population census were reported. The *Summary view* of 1830 included just one sentence on the scale of Irish population increase, and another asserting 'the frequent pressure of great distress among the labouring classes of society, and the practice of frequent and considerable emigration'.[12]

Malthus's harsh, uncompromising tone here presages the style of mainstream economists writing on prefamine Ireland. Analytically the argument seems to be that the increase in income associated with the discovery of the potato was all spent on marrying earlier and having and feeding a large family. No scope is left for better housing or clothes or education, or even a switch to some more expensive food. On the contrary, '(t)he great quantity of food which land will bear when planted with potatoes, and the consequent cheapness of labour supported by them, tends to raise than to lower the rents of land, and as far as rent goes, to keep up the price of the materials of manufactures and all other sorts of raw produce except potatoes. The indolence and want of skill which usually accompany such a state of things tend further to render all wrought commodities comparatively dear'. In other words, if wages are linked to the price of food, a drop in the latter will make workers *worse* off. Malthus's defence of the Corn Laws is based in part on the same reasoning: workers benefit because their wages are linked to (high) corn prices. Given the miserable state of the Irish poor when the *Essay* was written, and the apparent lack of any significant *sustained* increase in living standards in the decades before 1798, the model seems to fit Ireland better than most places. But the link between cheap food and squalid living in Ireland is asserted, not proven: as a great friend of Malthus's put it, 'sloth and rags are no more the concomitants of potatoes, than of wheat'.[13] Nor would today's Irish historians — any more than the Rev. Mr Broome — have much time for Malthus's one line interpretation of Ireland's 'year of liberty' and subsequent repression.

Much more moderate and sympathetic in tone are two review essays from his hand, published anonymously in the *Edinburgh Review* in 1808 and 1809. The two main works reviewed in them, both by Thomas Newenham, are still important primary sources for Irish historians. There is no evidence that Malthus did much special research for these reviews: on the contrary, they suggest a rather superficial knowledge of Irish history and conditions. Yet they cannot be dismissed in a discussion of Malthus and Ireland.[14]

Newenham is particularly well-known to Irish demographic historians for his careful and — as subsequent research confirms — quite accurate guess at the population of the island in 1804.[15] Malthus approved of Newenham's calculations, and accepted his suggestion of a fourfold increase in numbers during the eighteenth century as near the truth. He also considered Newenham's forecast of a population of over eight million by 1837 as plausible, and envisaged — if the potato diet continued — 'a much greater number in time'.[16] But inevitably, a 'less abundant supply of food' would eventually make itself felt, and the rate of population growth would taper off, 'as the gradual diminution of the real wages of the labouring classes of society, slowly, and almost insensibly, generates the habits necessary for an order of things in which the funds for the maintenance of labour are stationary'. What is striking in these *Edinburgh Review* articles is Malthus's quite benign prognosis of the adjustment process: the emphasis is very much on the 'preventive check', with a reduction in the 'habit of early marriages' and in mean family size. This is the anonymous Malthus, however; in public statements in the *Essay*, the *Principes of political economy*, and elsewhere, it is a different story.

Interestingly, Malthus in these *Edinburgh Review* articles explicitly rules out an eventuality such as the Great Famine. Change would be gradual: 'although it is quite certain that the population of Ireland cannot continue permanently to increase at its present rate, yet it is as certain that it will not *suddenly* come to a stop'. 'Je ne suis pas malthusien', Malthus might have replied to those disciples who interpreted the Famine as the classic Malthusian solution. Malthus, even at his most buoyant, however, would not have ruled out 'the periodical return of . . . seasons of distress' such as that of 1800-1 when, in Ireland and England, there was severe pressure on the food supply.[17]

The main theme in both reviews, totally absent in the *Essay*, is that the oppression of the Catholic majority in Ireland was conducive to a high birth rate: 'the humiliated Catholic, with no rank in society to support, has sought . . . only potatoes, milk, and a hovel, he has vegetated in the country of his ancestors, and overspread the land with his descendants'. Or, more generally: 'The causes which independently of soil and climate, have actually determined the chief food of the common people in the different kingdoms of Europe, seem to have been their political state'. For Malthus, a reduction in population growth in Ireland could be achieved by a shift in the fertility schedule. If the Catholics were given something to live for, 'as will make them look forward to other comforts beside the mere support of their families on potatoes', within a short space of time they would change their habit of marrying so early.[18] In these passages Malthus is much closer to critics such as Sadler, Bishop Doyle of Kildare and Leighlin, and Poulett Scrope, than in his other writings. However, an obvious implication of his model — that Catholic nuptiality and fertility was higher than Protestant — is left untested. The evidence of a softer side to Malthus is more important than the fact that he greatly overestimates the civil disabilities touching Catholics in 1808, and completely overlooks social and class differences within the Catholic community.

It must be also pointed out, however, that Malthus has no other substantive policy proposals to make. Indeed, perhaps his articles are best known in Ireland for their strong criticism of the interventionist proposals of Newenham. Newenham supported more generous corn bounties, an odd target for somebody soon to be regarded as political economy's main supporter of the Corn Laws.

II. THE POTATO, POVERTY, AND SUBSISTENCE CRISES

Was Ireland indeed 'a case study in malthusian economics'?[19] The temptation to follow majority historiographical tradition, and answer an unhesitating 'yes' is strong. But given the contrasting treatments in the *Edinburgh Review* and the *Essay,* perhaps the question is badly put. There was no ambiguity in Malthus's mind about over-population being the proximate cause of Irish poverty, but the law of diminishing returns is only part of the model. The adjustment forced by the two 'unequal powers' could come from either the positive or preventive check. There is a sense in which Malthusian views were flexible enough to be hard to refute![20] But did trends in Ireland before the Famine — over-reliance on the potato, youthful marriage, immiseration — augur subsistence crises of ever-increasing severity, and, *in extremis,* the Great Hunger itself? Or were there signs of the preventive check at work? The issues are important, but much necessary research remains to be done. The present contribution aims at provoking some caution or unease about the 'hard' Malthusian orthodoxy. The difficult issue of the law of diminishing returns is only very briefly addressed, at the end. Before proceeding, let us accept the conventional wisdom of declining living standards in the 1800-1845 period.

It seems right to begin with the potato, very much the 'villain of the piece' in Malthusian (or *malthean, pace* Maria Edgeworth) accounts of Ireland before 1845. Though a prolific crop and a filling food, its yield was judged to be unreliable, and to make matters worse, it could not be stored from one year to the next. A people whose normal fare was butcher's meat and corn could, it was said, fall back on potatoes in a bad year, but the potato-eater had nothing to fall back on. Historians are unsure about the timing of its introduction and diffusion in Ireland. Enough to report here that it probably made its appearance first in Munster as a seasonal garden crop in the early seventeenth century, fulfilling a role much like the carrot or turnip today. Mentioned several times in a section of *Pairlement Chloinne Tomáis* that was probably composed in the 1660s, it is significant that *Clann Tomáis* contemplated the ruin of their exploiters, the millers, by refusing to send them grain and boiling 'peas, beans, potatoes, and parsnips' instead.[21] Gradually the potato's keeping quality and yield were improved, and the root referred to as 'an Spáinneach' by an eighteenth century poet became truly the 'Irish' potato, lynchpin of Ireland's unique dietary and fodder revolution.[22] This revolution is commonly assumed to have initially reduced the risk of subsistence crises, producing a 'gap in famines' between the major catastrophe of 1740-1 and the early nineteenth century. According to Kenneth Connell, 'it is remarkable, but apparently true, that during eighty years of increasing dependence on the potato, even the rumblings of disaster were seldom heard'.[23] The potato did not bring higher material living standards, but it allowed people to marry young and to live longer. Subsequent over-reliance made for ever more frequent and more disastrous crises, however, In this view the serious failure of 1740 marked the temporary end of a high death rate regime, which resumed and worsened in the immediate prefamine decades. The Famine, or some major positive check like it, was thus foreseeable.

Further research in recent years has shown this story to be over-simplified. The evidence against a sudden end to famine after the 1740s is mainly literary; Charles O'Connor of Belanagare informing a Dublin correspondent in the spring of 1756 that in Connacht 'two thirds of the inhabitants are perishing for want of bread',[24] or a writer in the *Hibernian Magazine* in 1783 claiming that 'the emigration of the inhabitants of the kingdom to America has arrived to a most alarming excess, and threatens depopulation of this ill-governed country, where thousands are perishing for the want of the necessaries of life'.[25] But parish registers, admittedly sparse for the period, also highlight the persistence of mortality crises, and provide grounds for speculating that the most serious crises of the 1740-1800 period could have been *worse* than anything occurring between 1800 and the Great Famine. The nice correlation posited between increasing potato dependence and liability to famine is thus not proven.

It is unfortunate that the prefamine subsistence crises have been so little studied.[26] Retrospective analysis and comment have drawn a very bleak picture indeed. Best known, perhaps, is Surgeon William Wilde's account in the census report of 1851, which includes a catalogue of earlier famines. Wilde's report creates the impression that famine stalked the land almost annually in some part or other of the island between 1815 and 1845. It must be taken in conjunction with his report appended to the 1841 census, though. There starvation and famine-related deaths hardly rate a mention. The quantitative evidence produced by Wilde in 1841 suggests that sixty times as many people died of drowning, and ten times as many of intemperance, as of starvation during the 1830s. The census records 117 cases of death from starvation during the decade, compared to 139 from accidental poisoning and 197 from hanging. Now it is a safe bet that not all these 117 deaths from starvation were due to general subsistence crises: even after the Famine *individual* cases of starvation probably occurred. Against that, these deaths presumably do not include all those who died from diet-related causes,

Malthus and the pre-famine economy

though it is surely significant that Wilde does not discuss famine-related fevers either in his 1841 report.[27]

The other well-known survey worth noting here is Barker and Cheyne's account of the crisis of 1816-8. While primarily a medical account of the fever symptoms prevalent in those years, it does include an estimate of the mortality toll of the crisis. Barker and Cheyne's guesstimate is 65,000. This is miniscule when compared to either the Great Famine or the famine of 1740-1.[28] It is worth remembering too that 1816-8 were also the years of what John D. Post has called Europe's 'last great susbistence crisis'. Post's data suggest an excess mortality much greater in other parts of the continent than in Ireland. Indeed, the toll was enough in Switzerland, Austria, southern Germany, and northern Italy to wipe out all natural increase during these years:[29] Barker and Cheyne's figures indicate that Ireland lost only one-third of its natural increase during the same period. In the great famine of 1740-1, by contrast, Ireland and Norway were at the top of the European league. In sum, taking the long view, death from starvation and related ailments seems to have been more likely in 1750-1800 than in 1800-1845, and hardly of drastic proportions in the latter period. This is not what the simple Malthusian model predicts.

A related point: life expectancy in Ireland on the eve of the Famine may have been a little lower than in England, but the Irishman lived longer on than the average Frenchman or German.[30] Moreover, evidence that life expectancy was dropping before 1845 is lacking. I suspect a small rise, if anything: infant and child mortality at least seem to have *declined* in the prefamine decades. I am thinking here mainly of the impact of the campaign against smallpox which, in the east of the country at least, seems to have been significant by 1845.

Some further comment on the vulnerability of the potato seems appropriate. Historians disagree about it. The recent researches of Joel Mokyr mark a big step forward here.[31] Using French data as a proxy for non-existent Irish, he shows that pre-blight potato yields in northern and western France were more variable from year to year than either oats or wheat yields. Security, it would seem, was being traded off for volume. A reservation against using French data may be that a wetter and windier climate made potato yields in Ireland relatively less variable, or in other words, that Ireland had a comparative advantage in potatoes. The point is surely strengthened by a comparison of late nineteenth-century grain yields: the statistics suggest that the detrended coefficient of variation of oats yields was twice the French level in Ireland between 1871 and 1913. Against that, it might be urged that the increasing popularity of the notorious 'lumper' exacerbated the potato's riskiness in Ireland, to an extent not experienced elsewhere. For all we know, the yields of different potato varieties may have varied as much as those of any particular potato variety and grains.

Mokyr, like other critics of the potato, also emphasizes their high transport cost, which accentuated the problem of regional shortages. The potato's bulk no doubt militated against large-scale trade in it, and against regional specialization in its cultivation as well. The lack of storability is another common criticism, raised (and questioned) as long ago as 1823 by Maria Edgeworth in correspondence with David Ricardo.[32] These weighty objections against the potato imply that the millions relying on it were taking a big calculated risk each time they prepared their lazy-beds. Yet the indirect evidence, as we have seen, is hardly reassuring. If yields did not fluctuate fiercely, non-storability and non-transportability would not have been crucial drawbacks. Dare one speculate whether non-storability was an inherent problem, or simply something not worth bothering about? It is mildly curious that the Quechua, who gave Europe the potato, had developed a simple method of storing it for up to four years over a millenium before the Conquista,[33] though their success may simply reflect different soil and climatic conditions. As for transportability, Hoffman and Mokyr have produced strong evidence of the cost involved. Their analysis of data in Wakefield's *Account of Ireland, statistical and political* indicates that potatoes cost an extra 2.5 percent of their value for every mile they were transported. More research on regional price variations in good and bad years would be very enlightening. All I would like to point out here is that very detailed price data for 1839-45 suggest very little variation in regional price differentials from year to year. This could mean either no bad years in this period — despite Surgeon William Wilde — or adequate arbitrage.[34]

The potato failure caused what was arguably the greatest human tragedy in nineteenth-century Europe. This has earned it a fearsome reputation. The gift of hindsight is a mixed blessing for the historian, however. Those who stressed the benefits of the potato before 1845, both as human food and fodder crop, such as the famous 'Martin Doyle' who proclaimed them in verse, or the first holder of the Whately Chair of Political Economy, Mountifort Longfield, may well also have been right in their way, on the basis of the evidence available to them.[35] For insight into the prefamine economy, I would prefer a verse of doggerel from Martin Doyle any day to the far more influential contemporary or retrospective analyses of, say, Senior or Trevelyan. Longfield's vigorous defence, in a lecture delivered in Trinity College, Dublin in 1833, comes from an unexpected quarter, because 'potatoes', he admitted, 'appear to be in bad repute among political economists'. Discounting all the usual objections as unimportant, he insisted that 'if we look to the history of England, or any country at a time when it was as poor as Ireland is now, we shall find that dearths and famines were more frequent there and more tremendous in their effects than they have been in Ireland during the past thirty years'. Pigs, Longfield pointed out, are no more than stored-up potatoes. Nor could he understand how, when used as a subsidiary food, potatoes shield corn-eaters in time of dearth. 'Where are the potatoes to come from? They surely are not grown as a reserve for years of scarcity, to be thrown away in years of plenty. The ordinary cultivation will be the ordinary consumption, and there will not be an additional supply of potatoes to compensate a deficient harvest of corn.' For Longfield the strident attacks on the potato would be appropriate, 'if they eat men instead of feeding them'.[35]

III. THE PREVENTIVE CHECK

When Malthus wrote the *First essay* the population of Ireland was growing at over 1.5 percent annually, faster, perhaps, than anywhere else in Europe. During the 1820s, however, the rate of population increase had dropped to less than one percent, and between 1830 and the Famine, to about 0.5 percent. Most of the decline was due to rising emigration, but what of the rest? Was the death rate rising, by way of Malthusian warning, or the birth rate falling? Malthus himself evidently believed the former: in the 1820s, he surmised, 'prolificness, and the causes that prompt to marriage, are likely to be the same, but, in all probability, the mortality is greater'.[36] Alas, direct evidence is very scarce. The great census of 1841 provides only a still picture of the situation in that year, and the earlier censuses provide little comparative material. Historians have noted that the still picture of 1841 belies the prevalent contemporary notion of universal and very early marriage. The 1841 data can help too in projecting population backwards into the 1820s and 1830s, in order to search for changes in the birth rate. This technique combines information about the age structure of the population in 1841 and about emigrants leaving between 1821 and 1841, to estimate annual birth rates over the period. An exercise of this kind by Phelim Boyle and me suggests a *drop* in the birth rate from 42 to 37-38 per thousand over the two-decade period.[37]

A second source of evidence for demographic adjustment through the preventive check in these years refers only to the Dublin. By isolating first-time mothers from among the thousands who gave birth in the city's famous Rotunda Hospital in the prefamine period, evidence emerges for a rise in the female age at marriage between the 1810s and the 1840s. The rise between 1811 and 1840 is about 1.5 years, hardly sensational at first sight, but with impressive implications for family size. Irish marital fertility, it is generally conceded, was extremely high in the prefamine period, so high that the increase in marriage age will have meant 0.6 to 0.7 fewer children per average marriage.[38]

While the preventive check was thus playing its part before 1845 to an extent unsuspected by Malthusian commentators, it hardly needs pointing out that the people were also behaving in a manner Malthus would have approved of, when it came to the delicate matter of contraception. The late Kenneth Connell's case for this is *argumentum ex silentio:* 'the absence of reproof for what almost every writer of the age who touched on the subject regarded as a shameful sin, points to the conclusion that the influence of contraception may be disregarded'. The only *literary* references that I could find to contraception for the prefamine period occur in Brian Merriman's Cúirt an Mheánoíche. Merriman includes two for good measure. Here is Frank O'Connor's racy rendition of the first:

> I found her myself on the public road,
> On the naked earth with a bare backside
> And a Garus turfcutter astride!
> Is it any wonder my heart is failing,
> That I feel the end of the world is nearing,
> When, ploughed and sown to all men's knowledge,
> She can manage the child to arrive with marriage,
> And even then, put to the pinch,
> Begrudges Charity an inch;
> For, counting from the final prayer
> With the candles quenched and altar bare
> To the day when her offspring takes the air
> Is a full nine months with a week to spare?

The second, a call for an end to organized marriage, runs:

Malthus and the pre-famine economy

Leis sin ná hiarrsa a Riagain réaltach,
Meilleadh myriad le riail gan éifeacht,
Scaoil a chodladh *gan chochall gan chuibhreach*
Síol an bhodaigh 's an mhogallfhuil mhaíteach,
Scaoil fá chéile de réir nádúra
An siolbhach séad is an braon labúrtha.

Merriman experts are agreed that 'gan chochall gan chuibreach' (without sheath [hood], without restraint) can only mean something that would have quite upset Malthus! However, whether Merriman was reflecting custom in Munster in the 1770s, or merely borrowing images from poetry in other languages, is a nice question that I cannot answer. Leaving poetry aside, recent work with prefamine parish registers suggests that bridal pregnancies and illegitimate births were far rarer in Ireland than in England or on the Continent. Sean Connolly's analysis of the records of several parishes finds one premarital conception in ten; the average in contemporary rural England was about two in five. *A propos* Merriman, Connolly's reminder that the old Gaelic proclivity for coarse, earthy humour must not be mistaken for loose sexual behaviour is interesting.[39]

IV. EMIGRATION

Proponents of emigration as a solution to overpopulation, and more specifically to Ireland's problems, had in Malthus an unwilling and sceptical ally. Though prepared to support it as a once-off measure in special circumstances (e.g. in the wake of the peace of 1815), his considered belief was that while it 'might appear, on a first view of the subject, an adequate remedy', experience proved it to be but 'a slight palliative'. By the principle of population, the ensuing vacuum would soon be filled. True, Wilmot Horton had him dragged before the 1827 Select Committee on Emigration, and extracted support from him. But as subsequent correspondence amply shows, Malthus remained unconvinced of the lasting benefits of emigration.[40]

Chapter 2 of the *First essay* begins with an example depicting 'any spot on earth, this Island for instance', where the two 'unequal laws' are set to work unimpeded. In a matter of decades, of course, a massive surplus population has accumulated, 'totally unprovided for'. Yes, but why could it not move elsewhere? Malthus was evidently reluctant to admit this safety valve, for after a quick reference to the 'unhappiness' and 'strong subsisting causes of uneasiness' that follow emigration, he lamely switched analysis 'to the whole earth, instead of one spot'.[41] Nevertheless, Malthus was probably wrong to exclude emigration as a solution to overpopulation in smaller areas such as Ireland.

Emigration was a crucial element in Irish demographic change in the half-century or so before the Famine. Between 1815 and 1845 about 1.5 million Irish people left for good for Britain, Canada, and the United States, an exodus unprecedented in size until then. In those years Ireland accounted for one-third of the total trans-Atlantic migration. The emigrants left because of worsening economic conditions at home. Accepting for the sake of argument, that overpopulation was the root cause of the pressure on living standards, the outflow must then be treated as a form of 'preventive check'. The direct impact of the movement is clear enough: without it, Irish population would have continued to grow at a much faster rate. But emigration also affected the demographic structure of the population which remained at home.

The point here is that those who emigrated were not a representative sample of the population at large; the great majority were clustered in the biologically productive age-bracket, which must have reduced the birth rate. In addition, marriageable men were much more emigration-prone before the Famine than women, and this too must have affected the marriage rate in areas of high emigration, if only to a minor extent. By extension, the induced scarcity of potential husbands also reduced the birth rate.[42]

While emigration may thus be considered a sort of preventive check in the Irish context, arguably it operated with unequal efficiency within the island. Unfortunately, it would seem, the poorest areas supplied fewest emigrants. The available statistics suggest that the rate of emigration was lowest in Connacht and Munster. Whether a poverty trap prevented thousands from those provinces from leaving is a moot point. The high fare is often mentioned, but was in fact a small consideration compared to either some other costs of the passage, or the seasonal earnings of thousands of migrant workers, who could have remained on in Britain, but did not.

Irish historians, perhaps unduly influenced by Malthusian accounts, have sometimes been slow to recognize the size of the prefamine outflow. The image of peasant multitudes holding on, 'like sailors to the mass or hull of a wreck',[43] is made vivid by the carnage of the Great Famine. An alternative, more hopeful, interpretation of the record, is that emigration was growing and becoming an increasingly more realistic option for thousands in prefamine

Irish emigrant landing at Liverpool, by Erskine Nicol (by courtesy of the National Galleries of Scotland).

Ireland. Had *phytophthera infestans* stayed away, emigration would have increasingly done service as a preventive check.

V.   TRENDS IN THE PRE-FAMINE ECONOMY

The other key Malthusian premise, that Ireland was becoming progressively poorer because population was getting larger and larger, is very difficult to test, but there is much suggestive evidence for it. In the prefamine period, it is generally agreed that living standards were falling; moreover, they were apparently falling most where population grew most. Turning one's mind's eye first to upland or boggy potato patches in Mayo or Kerry, and then to snug mixed farms in Carlow or Wexford, one supposes that poverty was greatest in areas where the land-labour ratio was lowest. But it is perhaps not quite that simple.

One caveat is that the Malthusian concern with the movement of an average — the land-labour ratio — obscures an important feature of life in prefamine Ireland, and in many less developed countries, a very unequal access to the land resource. Even in prefamine Connacht, where the smallholding problem was gravest and almost two in three landholders scraped a living out of ten acres or less, the average amount of cultivable land per landholder was over twenty acres. The situation in a place like Wexford was better not *only* because there was more land per head, but because the size distribution of farms was markedly more equal. The Malthusian — or neo-Malthusian — riposte to this objection is presumably that overpopulation itself increased inequality. The poor were largely responsible for the 'early and improvident marriages' which produced undue population pressure. The point is familiar to students of development economics.

Given the utter impossibility in 1800 or 1845 of the kind of redistribution sought by reformers later on in the century — and sometimes successfully achieved by revolutionary means in the twentieth — the Malthusian view has a depressing cogency. But Malthus must not make us ignore inequality in a diagnosis of poverty: even during the Great Famine unequal *access* to food exacerbated the problem of overall food shortage. Too often, not least during the Famine, 'overpopulation' excused events which might have been prevented by a little more charity, private or public. Malthus's misleading tendency to treat the Catholic majority as an undifferentiated potato-eating mass has already been noted: perhaps it was because he thought the scope for redistribution

Malthus and the pre-famine economy

to be trivial.[44] But the 'poor' who concerned Malthus, and who alarmed many policy-makers in the prefamine period, were only the bottom thirty or forty percent of the population, and their combined incomes came to no more than 10-15 percent of national income.

The Malthusian approach ignores entirely another possible factor behind the decline in prefamine living standards, the effect on the landless of the collapse of domestic or proto-industry. A few statistics based on the 1821 and 1841 censuses may help here. In the case of badly-hit Mayo, for example, the share of the labour force *not* primarily dependent on agriculture for their livelihood dropped from 58 percent in 1821 to 36 percent in 1841. The numbers suggest that as much — maybe even *more* — of the fall in the land-labour ratio there is accounted for by the shift from tertiary and secondary sector employment than by population increase. The same could be said of many other areas, especially in the north and west. Now it is perfectly true that the competition which ruined much domestic industry in the 1820s and 1830s also improved Ireland's terms of trade, and probably increased aggregate income. But this was little consolation to the landless, the demand for whose services dropped. Initially at least, the main beneficiaries in Ireland of British industrialization — if we exclude the north-east — were the stronger farmers and the landlords.[45]

These points may be regarded as no more than anti-Malthusian skirmishing. Whether productivity change in Irish agriculture was too slow to outpace the law of diminishing returns — a central point — is still not proven. Neither accounts of the diffusion of new crops and better landlord management, on the one hand, nor evidence that farm labourers' living standards were under constant pressure in the prefamine decades, on the other, are substitutes for hard estimates of output and input trends. My guess is that agricultural output about doubled between 1800 and 1845. If so, output growth outpaced population; but the occupational shift caused by the decline of Irish industry was partly responsible for this. Besides, the *rate* of expansion may have been diminishing over the period. As far as the eighteenth century goes, we are in statistical limbo: the contours of population growth have been established with some confidence, but little is known about variations over time and across regions in real income. Money wage series may be obtained, but when it comes to the price level all one can do is lamely invoke purchasing power parity, and use British data. On that basis, my guess is that real wages did not change much over the century. But the welfare aspects of early marriage and greater life expectancy must not be overlooked.[46]

In sum, time series data offers little against which to test Malthus. The great progress that has been made in Irish economic history during the last few decades has yielded much demographic and trade data, but too little on factor payments, income distribution, and prices. *Faute de mieux,* looking at postfamine trends may provide a lead here. Between 1845 and the mid-1870s, a drop of 35-40 percent in the labour force produced a drop of 20-25 percent in agricultural net output. Let us suppose — it is a common implicit assumption in agrarian history — that a declining labour force is less likely to thwart technical change than a rising one. In that case, the law of diminishing returns could hardly have been countered sufficiently before 1845 to prevent a drop in the marginal contribution of labour. The lack of aggregate time-series data precludes a firmer conclusion. But a full-scale attack on this aspect of the Malthusian model, by a different approach, has been launched by Joel Mokyr of Northwestern University in his recent book *Why Ireland starved.*[47] Skirting the data problem by using the thirty-two counties of Ireland as so many observations of the country at different stages of potential population pressure, he finds that the prime Malthusian variable, the land-labour ratio, adds little insight to the explanation of Irish poverty before the Famine. Mokyr's *tour de force* argues this and much else. I suggest that the issue is best left to a reading of the book and the debate and controversy that it will undoubtedly spark off.

In conclusion: Malthus himself had little profound to say about prefamine Ireland specifically. The plausibility of the Malthusian framework nonetheless has captivated and convinced generations of commentators. Plausibility is not enough, however. I have attempted to provide instances where Malthus's guesses were off-target. But 'Population Malthus' will continue to provide a context for, and spur further research on, the prefamine economy.

Notes

1. Thomas Flanagan, *The year of the French* (London, 1979), pp 500-1. See also n. 11 below.

2. John K. Galbraith, *The age of uncertainty* (Boston, 1977), pp 37-8; William Petersen, *Malthus* (London, 1979), pp 102-10; David Grigg, *Population growth and agrarian change* (Cambridge, 1981), pp 115-40.

3. L. M. Cullen, *Life in Ireland* (London, 1969), p. 142.

4. Nassau William Senior, *Journals, essays and conversations relating to Ireland* (London, 1868), vol. 2, pp 2-3.

Malthus and the pre-famine economy

5. Oliver McDonagh, *The nineteenth century novel and Irish social history: some aspects* (Dublin, n.d.), p. 7.

6. Kenneth H. Connell, *Irish peasant society* (Oxford, 1968), p. 116.

7. McDonagh, *loc.sit.*

8. Robert D. C. Black, *Economic thought and the Irish question* (Cambridge, 1960), pp 18, 91, 203-4; Senior, *op.cit.* especially vol. 1.

9. Thomas R. Malthus, *An essay on the principle of population, as it affects the future improvement of society* (London, 1798); all references here are to the Pelican version (Harmondsworth, 1970).

10. Malthus, *An essay . . .*, Everyman edition, vol. i, pp 277-8. The passage is quoted in Patricia James, *Population Malthus* (London, 1979), pp 145-6, a brilliant introduction to the man and his ideas.

11. Flanagan, *op.cit.*, p. 501; Rev. William Richardson, DD, quoted in P. James, *op.cit.*, pp 146-7. Flanagan had Broome reading the 1803 edition in 1798 — but must be allowed the artistic licence to do so.

12. James, *op.cit.* notes the changes in the 1826 edition. Malthus's *Summary view of the principle of population* (London, 1830), is also reprinted in the Pelican edition of the *Essay*. Ireland is referred to on p. 236.

13. Malthus, *Essay*, 7th edition (London, 1872), p. 324; David Ricardo in P. Sraffa (ed.), *The works and correspondence of David Ricardo*, vol. ix (Cambridge, 1952), p. 239; W. D. Grampp, 'Malthus on Money Wages and Welfare', *American Economic Review*, 46 (1956), 924-36.

14. Malthus, 'Newenham and others on the state of Ireland', *Edinburgh Review*, July 1808, and 'Newenham on the state of Ireland', *Edinburgh Review*, April 1809: both articles have been reprinted in Bernard Semmel (ed.), *Occasional papers of T. R. Malthus on Ireland, population, and political economy* (New York, 1963), pp 32-71, and further references will be to this source.

15. On Newenham, see Joseph Lee (ed.), *Irish population before the nineteenth century* (London, 1973), editor's introduction, and H. Gribbon, 'Thomas Newenham' in M. Goldstrom and L. E. Clarkson (eds.), *Population, economy, and society: essays in memory of the late K. H. Connell* (Oxford, 1981), pp 231-48. In Newenham's *An inquiry into the progress etc. of the population of Ireland* (London, 1805), there is a reference (p. 5) to Malthus as a 'writer of considerable abilities and erudition', and an admission that his 'most valuable work . . . did not fall into (Newenham's) hands, until after the printing of these pages had commenced'.

16. Semmel, p. 42.

17. Semmel, p. 42. On the shortage of 1800 see T. R. Malthus, *An investigation of the cause of the present high price of provisions* (London, 1800).

18. Semmel, pp. 45, 48, 50, 63, 66.

19. Barbara L. Solow, *The land question and the Irish economy 1870-1903* (Cambridge, Mass., 1971), p. 196.

20. Compare Mark Blaug, *Economic theory in retrospect*, 3rd ed. (Cambridge, 1978), pp 76-9.

21. N. J. A. Williams (ed.), *Pairlement Chloinne Tomáis* (Dublin, 1981), p. 63.

22. By far the best extended study of the potato in prefamine Ireland is Austin Bourke's unpublished doctoral dissertation, 'Potato, blight, weather and the great Irish famine', (National University of Ireland, 1965). Joel Mokyr, 'Irish history with the potato', *Irish Economic and Social History*, 8 (1981), pp 8-29, is a good introduction to the debate on the potato's place in Irish economic history.

23. Kenneth Connell, *The population of Ireland 1750-1845* (Oxford, 1950), p. 146.

24. Catherine C. Ward and Robert E. Ward (eds.), *The letters of Charles O'Conor of Belanagare*, vol. I (Ann Arbor, 1980), p. 14. See also W. H. Lecky, *Irish life in the eighteenth century*, i (London, 1892), p. 461.

Cormac Ó Gráda

25. Quoted by Wilde in the 1851 census report, *Tables of death*, p. 151 — see fn. 27. See also *Faulkner's Dublin Journal*, 'Letter by S.L.', April 30, 1757; Samuel Burdy, *The life of the late Rev. Philip Skelton* (Dublin, 1792), pp 171-4, 196-7. I owe these references to Dr David Dickson of Trinity College, Dublin.

26. See, however, David Dickson, 'Famine in Ireland, 1700-1775: A review', paper presented to the Economic and Social History Society of Ireland Conference, Derry, September 1981.

27. *The census of Ireland for the year 1851*, Part V: *Tables of deaths*, vol. 1, *containing the report, tables of pestilences, and analysis of the tables of deaths*, [2087-I], H.C. 1856, xxix, 261; *Report of the Commissioners appointed to take the census of Ireland for the year 1841*, [504] H.C. 1843, xxiv, 1.

28. F. Barker and J. Cheyne, *An account of the rise, progress and decline of the fever late epidemical in Ireland* (Dublin, 1821); Stuart Daultrey, David Dickson, and C. Ó Gráda, 'Eighteenth-century Irish Population: Old Sources and New Speculations', *Journal of Economic History*, xli (1981), pp 626-7.

29. John D. Post, *The last great subsistence crisis in the western world* (Baltimore, 1977), pp 108-22.

30. Phelim P. Boyle and C. Ó Gráda, 'Fertility trends, excess mortality and the great Irish famine', unpublished working paper, U.C.D. Dec. 1982.

31. J. Mokyr, 'Uncertainty and prefamine Irish agriculture', in T. Devine and D. Dickson (eds.). *Ireland and Scotland: essays in comparative economic and social history 1650-1900* (Edinburgh, 1983); E. Hoffman and J. Mokyr, 'Peasants, potatoes, and poverty: transactions costs in prefamine Ireland', Center for Mathematical Studies in Economics and Management Science, Northwestern University, Discussion Paper No. 474, April 1981.

32. P. Sraffa (ed.), *The works and correspondence of David Ricardo* (Cambridge, 1960), especially vol. IX, pp 230-2, 237-9, 252-5.

33. Robert E. Rhoades, 'The incredible potato', *National Geographic Magazine*, May 1982, pp 673-6.

34. Hoffman and Mokyr, pp 35-9; *Report on the highest price of potatoes in the various market towns in Ireland per bushel or per stone in the week ending 24 January, for the last seven years, as well as can be estimated*, [110], 1846, xxxvi, 489.

35. 'M. Doyle', quoted in Robert McKay, *An anthology of the potato* (Dublin, 1961), p. 58; M. Longfield, *Lectures on political economy* (Dublin, 1834), pp 249-56.

36. Malthus's evidence to *Select committee on emigration*, [550] H.C. 1826-7, v, 311-27.

37. Boyle and Ó Gráda, 'Fertility trends'.

38. C. Ó Gráda, 'Prefamine Dublin's demography: the evidence from the Rotunda records', paper presented at the Economic and Social History Society of Ireland Conference, Cork, September 1982.

39. Kenneth H. Connell, *The population of Ireland 1750-1845* (Oxford, 1950), pp 49-50; Brian Merriman, *Cúirt an Mheánoíche* (edited by Dáithí Ó hUaithne) (Dublin, 1968), lines 457-476, 629-35; *Cúirt an Mheonoíche* (edited by Liam P. Ó Murchú) (Dublin, 1982), pp 31, 36, 55; translation in Brendan Kennelly (ed.), *The Penguin book of Irish verse*, 2nd ed. (Harmondsworth, 1981), pp 103, 107. O'Connor mistranslated the second extract. I am grateful to Liam P. Ó Murchú of University College Cork, editor of the most recent (1982) edition of *An Chúirt*, for drawing my attention to Merriman's references. On illegitimacy and bridal pregnancy, see S. J. Connolly, *Priests and people in pre-famine Ireland* (Dublin, 1982), pp 186-91.

40. R. N. Ghosh, 'Malthus on emigration and colonization: letters to Wilmot-Horton', *Economica*, February 1963; R. N. Ghosh, 'The colonization controversy: R. J. Wilmot-Horton and the classical economists', *Economica*, Nov. 1964; H. J. M. Johnston, *British emigration policy 1815-1830: shovelling out paupers* (Oxford, 1972), especially pp 2-3, 11-3, 109-139.

Malthus and the pre-famine economy

41. Malthus, *First essay*, pp 74-5.

42. C. Ó Gráda, 'Across the briny ocean: some thoughts on Irish emigration to America, 1800-1850', in Devine and Dickson (eds.), *op.cit.*

43. O. McDonagh, *A pattern of government growth 1800-60: the Passenger Acts and their enforcement* (London, 1961), pp 24-7. As McDonagh urges, the 'surprise' is that the outflow was not larger and growing faster.

44. It is also true that on policies touching the redistribution of wealth, Malthus's views were profoundly conservative. See e.g. *The principles of political economy*, 2nd ed. (London, 1836), pp 376-82. On the link between population growth and inequality see e.g. M. Ahluwalia, 'Inequality, poverty and development', *Journal of Development Economics* 3 (1976), 316, 325-7.

45. The implicit model is that S. Hymer and S. Resnick, 'A model of an agrarian economy with non-agrarian activities', *American Economic Review*, 59 (1969), pp 493-506.

46. In the terminology of Ronald Lee, eighteenth-century Ireland's capacity for 'population absorption' was quite high. See R. Lee, 'A historical perspective on economic aspects of the population explosion: the case of preindustrial England' in Richard Easterlin (ed.), *Population and economic change in developing countries* (Chicago, 1980), pp 517-25.

47. Allen and Unwin, 1983. See also J. Mokyr, 'Malthusian models and Irish history', *Journal of Economic History* XL (1980), pp 159-66.

0322
Cairnes, John Elliot
Mill, John Stuart

96-119

John Elliot Cairnes, John Stuart Mill and Ireland: some problems for political economy

by T. A. Boylan and T. P. Foley

In the early years of their friendship John Stuart Mill wrote that John Elliot Cairnes was 'one of the ablest of the distinguished men who have given lustre to the much-calumniated Irish colleges, as well as to the chair of Political Economy that Ireland owes to the enlightened public spirit of Archbishop Whately'.[1] It is appropriate that Cairnes, the main focus of our paper, should be reassessed in a series of lectures commemorating the founding of the Whately chair. Part of our purpose is to suggest that Cairnes's contribution to economic thought, though almost universally acknowledged as honourable, has been seriously underestimated.

This offering is the first-fruit of a larger study of the life and works of Cairnes, and is also part of a more general study of Irish political economy in the 19th century. We will begin by giving a brief life of Cairnes, noting especially his friendship with Mill. The main body of the paper will be divided into two parts. The first will deal with Cairnes's changing views on the state of Ireland with special emphasis on his contributions to Mill's understanding of Irish society. In general, this part of the paper will be modestly descriptive. In the other main section of the paper we will examine briefly Cairnes's contribution to economic thought and policy in the context of his reputation as conventionally perceived. We will then suggest how some, at least, of his contributions to political economy can be ascribed to his Irish experience. This will lead to a broadening of the paper to include some remarks of a preliminary and tentative kind on the fraught relationship between Ireland and the science, or alleged science, of political economy.

I

John Elliot Cairnes was born at Castlebellingham, County Louth, in December 1823 into a brewing family.[2] As a child he was considered so dull as to be even unfit to attend university. He incurred paternal displeasure by declining to enter the family business. However, he entered Trinity College Dublin in 1842, emerging

96

John Elliot Cairnes (by courtesy of University College, Galway).

in 1848 complete with the B.A. degree. He collected the M.A. in
1854. William Nesbitt, Professor of Latin and later of Greek at
Queen's College Galway, had turned Cairnes's attention to the
study of political economy and urged him to compete for the
Whately professorship. Cairnes was successful and became the sixth
incumbent of the chair in 1856, holding it for the full five-year
tenure. In 1859 he was appointed to the chair of jurisprudence and
political economy at Queen's College Galway, an appointment he
held until 1870. In 1866 he was appointed to the professorship of
political economy at University College London. Thus he held
joint-professorships in Galway and Dublin between 1859 and 1861
and in London and Galway between 1866 and 1870. Because of
ill-health he resigned the London professorship in 1872, having
already vacated his Galway chair two years previously.

It is worth noting that Cairnes was unique among the holders of
the Whately chair of his time in that while trained as a lawyer — he
was called to the Bar in 1857 — he never seriously practised law
nor engaged in any other occupation. He was from the beginning a
full-time academic economist; indeed he was one of the first professional economists in Great Britain and Ireland.

II

Cairnes and Mill first met at the Political Economy Club in London
in 1859[3] and from then on they exchanged letters regularly. Cairnes
was to become 'perhaps the most highly valued' of all of Mill's later
correspondents.[4] The editors of the definitive Toronto edition of
Mill's correspondence have claimed that 'more than any other of
Mill's correspondence except perhaps that with Carlyle . . . both
sides of the Cairnes-Mill series deserve publication together'.[5] Mill
himself wrote to Cairnes declaring, with reference to their letters,
that they were 'like . . . the philosophic correspondence in which
the thinkers of the 16th and 17th centuries used to compare notes
and discuss each other's opinions before and after publication — of
which we have seen many interesting specimens in the published
works of Descartes'.[6]

Our focus in this paper, however, is on the Cairnes-Mill correspondence as it related to Ireland. Mill had long been interested in
Irish affairs, and his writings on Ireland could be divided into three
phases. The first goes back to 1846-47 when Mill abandoned his
work on the *Principles of political economy* for six months to write a
series of articles — forty-three in all — for the *Morning Chronicle*

J. E. Cairnes, J. S. Mill and Ireland

between October 1846 and January 1847. These were primarily concerned with discussing the implications of the Famine and particularly Thornton's proposals for the reclamation of waste lands. The second phase is represented in the various editions of his *Principles* — it went through seven between 1848 and 1871. The third phase is to be found in his pamphlet, *England and Ireland,* published in 1868. In this section we will examine the writings of Cairnes on Ireland to discover to what extent, if any, they could be said to have influenced J. S. Mill.

The year 1864 must be taken as the most appropriate starting point for our discussions. In that year Cairnes published his first article on Ireland anonymously in the *Edinburgh Review,*[7] and also planned to write a volume of essays on Ireland.[8] In the same year Mill set about the revision of the fifth edition of his *Principles of political economy.* From their correspondence of 1864, which mainly concerned the revision of the *Principles,* it is possible to trace the evolution of Cairnes's thought on Ireland. His initial reaction to Mill's invitation, in October 1864, 'to make any improvement' in his treatment of Ireland in the fifth edition 'that you can suggest, and especially to know if there is anything which you think it would be useful to say on the present state of Ireland',[9] was one of overall agreement with Mill's position on Ireland. In that edition Mill had displayed extraordinary optimism when he argued that due to the large decrease of the population and the work of the Encumbered Estates Act, which Mill termed the 'greatest of boons ever conferred on [Ireland] by any government', made, according to Mill, 'the introduction, on a large scale, of the English agricultural system for the first time possible in that country'. He concluded that 'Ireland, therefore, was not now in a condition to require what are called heroic remedies'.[10] Whatever Mill may have meant by 'heroic remedies', peasant proprietorship was not now seen as being among them. While Mill conceded that peasant proprietorship was desirable, it was 'no longer indispensable'.[11] Cairnes, apart from making a number of comments about the need for further reforms, agreed totally with Mill and clearly shared Mill's basic optimism about the future.[12]

Later that year — in reply to a query from Mill concerning the state of the cottier class[13] — we get further insight into Cairnes's perception of the problem. Writing from Galway on 6 December 1864, and promising a fuller and more accurate reply, Cairnes believed that there 'is no doubt that the class of cottier tenants has been immensely reduced in Ireland and that the causes now in operation are tending rapidly to its entire extinction'. However Cairnes felt that the problem of over-population still remained, and that the means of raising the standard of living of 'the mass of the Irish working population' would mean 'dissociating them altogether from their present mode of life'. The methods envisaged by Cairnes for this dissociation included the provision of small parcels of land, the development of economic activity outside agriculture, along with continued emigration. Whatever Cairnes may have felt about the effectiveness of these measures in the future, he was under no illusions as to what had been already achieved. He argued that up to the present at least, the extent to which cottiers had been 'converted into labourers, no good has been done', and that were it not for emigration he felt that it could be 'confidently predicted that within a generation the [population] would be reduced once more to the starvation point'. Indeed Cairnes argued that 'even with the emigration I feel very sanguine it will not be avoided'.[14] Clearly, even within the short period between October and December 1864, Cairnes had adopted a considerably more pessimistic position with regard to the future of the cottier and labouring classes. Interestingly, when Mill replied to this particular letter he stated that, with respect to Ireland, he would '. . . cancel all I had newly written on that subject, and wait for the further communication you kindly promise'.[15]

This 'further communication' comprised the *Notes on the state of Ireland (1864)*, which were sent by Cairnes in December.[16] These *Notes* contained a more elaborate articulation of Cairnes's position in relation to Ireland. Cairnes addressed himself to four principal questions or themes. These included the 'extensive reductions' of cottierism in Ireland, the prospects of the farming class immediately above the cottier class, the arguments in favour of a peasant proprietorship, and the problems of getting the land into the hands of the actual cultivators. In this paper we will concentrate on two aspects of the material contained in the *Notes* — firstly, on those parts which were used by Mill in the revised edition of his *Principles*, and secondly on Cairnes's discussion of peasant proprietorship in which he disagreed fundamentally with Longfield's position.

The first aspect of Cairnes's *Notes* incorporated by Mill into his revised *Principles* included Cairnes's analysis of the reasons for the reduction in cottierism.[17] The contributing factors to this process identified by Cairnes included the impact of free trade, which was instrumental in the transformation of the agricultural economy from tillage to pasture[18] and the Famine, with its associated change in the attitude of the landlords who had learned that cottierism was 'as ruinous to them as it is demoralizing to the peasantry'.[19] In addition Cairnes argued that the attitude to the new proprietors, who had acquired land through the Landed Estates Court, resulted in land being viewed primarily as an investment and from this perspective cottiers were 'an abomination'.[20] Finally, Cairnes argued that the increased contact with America and other 'new countries' facilitated continued large-scale emigration.[21] The combined impact of these factors, concluded Cairnes, would result in such an enormous reduction in cottierism as to render it unimportant.[22] What Cairnes provided here for Mill was a systematization of the reasons for the expected reduction in cottierism, something which was missing from the fifth but which Mill included in his new edition. However Cairnes's contribution to this topic did not end here. He made a number of important qualifications, which Mill reproduced in full in the revised edition. These concerned the 'influence exercised on land tenure through the commercial ideas of the new proprietory', whom Cairnes felt were unsuitable as landlords precisely because of their commercial ideas.[23] Cairnes's other qualification concerned the role of middlemen, who in their desire to get cottiers as tenants, neutralized the anxiety of the landlords to get rid of cottiers.[24]

The second major area where Mill relied on Cairnes's material concerned the position and prospects of the farming class immediately above cottiers — those holding 15 to 30 acres. With respect to this class, Cairnes argued that the accumulation of private balances and deposits in the banks between 1840 and 1861, which had risen three-fold over this period, represented the accumulated savings of this small farming class. Cairnes provided a succinct summary of the port-folio options available to the small farming class when he commented that 'for the most part they look upon the bank as the only alternative to the thatch', and concluded that 'notwithstanding the symptoms of poverty that still everywhere abound . . . wealth is growing among this class'. This conclusion prompted Cairnes to raise the question, why, given the backward state of agriculture, were their savings not invested for the improvement of their farms? Cairnes felt that the solution to this problem was 'to be sought in many directions', but went on to state that 'security of tenure' was 'an indispensable condition'. In fact Cairnes, in a footnote, argued for what he termed 'substantial security of tenure', which was not to be equated with the 'wholesale confiscation of property in favour of existing cultivators'.[25] On the general topic of security of tenure, Cairnes expressed the opinion that 'Longfield's treatment of this project seemed to me, as a matter of speculation, to be profoundly fallacious', but he did not disagree with Longfield's assessment of the 'practical mischief which constant agitation of these schemes produces in the unsettling of people's minds'.[26]

It was in the course of his examination of the position of the small farming class that Cairnes raised the question of the prospects of a class of peasant proprietors arising in Ireland. It was on this issue that his differences with Longfield became most pronounced, and it is of some interest to examine briefly Cairnes's thinking on this issue. Longfield's position on peasant proprietorship rested on three basic assumptions:

(i)   that in Ireland wherever 'substantial interests exist in land, the owner of such interest almost invariably sublets',

(ii) that 'the natural disposition of the Irish people is careless improvident given to dash and show — in a word the opposite in all respects of that mental type which is the characteristic of peasant proprietors, and which seems to be indispensable to the keeping up of peasant proprietors',

(iii) that 'the peasant proprietor regime belongs to an earlier and primitive conditions of society' and could therefore be expected to disintegrate under the impact of economic and social development.[27]

Cairnes disagreed with Longfield on all three assumptions and argued cogently against them as follows:

(i)   with respect to Longfield's first position, Cairnes argued that the tendency to sublet was 'the natural and inevitable consequences of former social and political conditions', conditions which Cairnes felt had more affinity with the ethics of 'feudal and medieval' arrangements, but were now rapidly passing away as far as the landlord class was concerned. If this was true for the landlords, would it not, argued Cairnes, trickle down to the classes below them, thereby neutralizing the 'landlord passion' in the lower classes?

(ii) in relation to Longfield's second position, Cairnes accepted that 'no doubt the Irish disposition is careless and improvident' but he refused to accept the inevitability of Longfield's position, and raised the question as to whether we are 'to suppose that these qualities are ineradicable?' Cairnes argued that the presence of these dispositions could be explained historically, and in order to eradicate them it was all the more necessary to provide for peasant proprietorship. Cairnes himself stated his position as follows: 'regarded from this point of view, peasant proprietorship appears to me to be exactly the specific for the prevailing Irish disease.'

(iii) Cairnes argued against Longfield's third position by drawing on the evidence from such countries as France and the northern states of America to demonstrate that peasant proprietorship was the prevailing form of land tenure. In fact Cairnes viewed the English system of tenure, 'as an exception to the prevailing order of democratic progress than as indicating the rule'. This was a theme Cairnes was to return to again in the future. Even if Longfield's argument was conceded, Cairnes still felt that it would be 'good policy to encourage this system as a transitional expedient to help Ireland forward in its course'. While Mill did not make use of this material, it reflected clearly the direction Cairnes's thinking was soon to take.[28]

In contrast, an area where Mill did make extensive use of Cairnes's *Notes* concerned the problem of the land 'getting in any large extent into the hands of the actual cultivators'.[29] On this issue Cairnes felt that to a limited extent 'this has been, or at least was realised'. What Cairnes appears to be concerned with here are the different factors which influenced the price of land. His principal concern was with the high cost of the conveyance of land through the Landed Estates Court. This represented a barrier to the purchase of smaller portions of land, thereby hindering the downward mobility of land. As long as this situation prevailed, Cairnes felt that 'the experiment of peasant proprietorship . . . cannot fairly be tried'.[30] What Mill had called the 'greatest boon ever conferred on Ireland by any Government' became, according to Cairnes's analysis, a less than satisfactory mechanism for the transfer of land.

Writing to Cairnes on 5 January 1865, Mill, referring to the *Notes*, commented that 'They are a complete Essay on the state and prospects of Ireland, and so entirely satisfactory that they leave me nothing to think of except how to make the most of them'.[31] What differences, one may ask, did the material contained in the *Notes* make to Mill's thinking on Ireland? Three areas can be identified. In the first place, Mill dropped all reference in the sixth edition to the possibility of the English agricultural system becoming successfully established in Ireland. This is of some significance, and could be interpreted as representing the beginning of a major shift in Mill's view on the Irish question, particularly given Cairnes's argumentation against Longfield on the issue of peasant proprietorship. Secondly, while remaining over-optimistic with respect to the disappearance of the cottier-class, the inclusion of Cairnes's qualifications which highlighted certain countervailing tendencies, provided a more modified version of Mill's position, as contained in the fifth edition. Thirdly, Mill's continued extravagant claims for the efficiency of the Landed Estates Court as a mechanism for the transfer of land was qualified as a result of Cairnes's identification of the problem of the high cost of conveyancing in the Court, qualifications which Mill reproduced in full.[32] On balance, while the changes incorporated into the sixth edition reflect a relationship of total reliance by Mill on Cairnes, there is no evidence, at this stage, of a fundamental shift in Mill's position. This was to come later in *England and Ireland,* influenced, we will argue, by Cairnes's writing on Ireland in the course of 1865.

It soon became clear to Cairnes that facilitating land transfers would do little to solve Ireland's problems. Writing to Mill on 24 January 1865, he stated that 'something, but not very much, may be effected towards cheapening the process by a registration of titles on Lord Westbury's or Mr. Torren's plan, that might be done by a Register of Deeds; but that to accomplish anything effective — I mean that would meet the requirements of Ireland — more radical remedies are necessary'.[33] In the meantime Cairnes had been requested by Judge Longfield to give evidence before the Parliamentary Committee which had been established to inquire into tenant-right, and we know that Cairnes gave his 'conditional assent'.[34] At this time also he wrote a number of articles for the *Daily News* on the land question in Ireland.[35] But Cairnes's most significant writings on Ireland were undoubtedly a series of nine articles entitled 'Ireland in transition' which he contributed to the *Economist* between 9 September and 4 November 1865. These articles are perhaps best seen in terms of the 'state of the nation' debate which D. C. Heron had inaugurated in May 1862, and which included contributions by Longfield, Ingram, Hancock, and indeed Cairnes himself in his article in the *Edinburgh Review*.[36]

The *Economist* articles constituted a plea for peasant proprietors, and a rejection of the view that the only possible or desirable future for Irish agriculture lay in the creation of large farms based on the English or Scottish model. At the level of policy the articles modestly set forth a scheme of tenant-compensation, compatible with the principles of free-trade, to promote peasant proprietorship. But this scheme was justified on the basis of a searching critique of the accepted theory of private property in land. This represented a radical shift in Cairnes's thinking. His critique rested on a number of basic premises. Land, he argued, differed from the other agents of production in a number of respects:

J. E. Cairnes, J. S. Mill and Ireland

(i) It was 'absolutely indispensable to the most human needs, and at the same time was absolutely limited in quantity'.

(ii) Unlike the great mass of commodities, it was not 'the creation of any man's industry'.

(iii) In the productive process it could be 'greatly improved or deteriorated according to the treatment it receives'.[37]

For Cairnes, individual property in land was not only different from other forms of property, it was subordinate to them, in that it did not derive from 'that act which forms in the last resort the natural title deed to almost all other wealth — human labour'. In fact, the cultivator's right to the value he added to land was for this reason more fundamental than the landlord's rights to the property in his land. Cairnes argued that this 'conflict of principles' had already occurred in Ireland, and in this conflict the labourer had the 'paramount claim'.[38] For Cairnes, the 'practical exigencies of Ireland' were demanding 'a more thorough analysis and a larger theory of the facts' of land tenure. Not only was the English agricultural model totally inappropriate to Ireland, but what he called 'English theory' was at variance with 'Irish ideas' about landed property, and did not explain Irish 'fact'. He viewed the 'peculiar Irish notion' respecting landed property as being, paradoxically, a more universal phenomenon than the 'approved doctrine' of the English classical position, a notion which had 'a solid foundation in fact — a foundation of which the accepted theory takes no account'. Cairnes rejected the English doctrine of 'open competition and contract as the remedy of all social disorders arising from land tenure', and claimed that the relationship between landlord and tenant was not an ordinary contract but one that demanded 'from the State a large supervision and control'.[39] In a later article in the *Economist*, he argued that Fortescue's Irish Land Bill embodied 'a new principle in English legislation . . . the assertion in a general form of the subordination of the landlord's right in his property to the public welfare'. This principle was in Cairnes's view 'an entirely sound one, and one of which the recognition is absolutely indispensable to an effective dealing with the pressing requirement of Ireland',[40] and in a letter to Mill, in May 1867, he expressed the hope that the bill would be passed 'as affording a recognition of the principles of the limited character of the landlord's property in the soil'.[41]

In a letter of 6 January 1866, Mill informed Cairnes that he had read several of the *Economist* articles and had 'admired them greatly', and added that the 'generalities of the question have perhaps never before been so well stated' as in Cairnes's first article.[42] Cairnes thanked Mill for the 'very handsome terms' in which he expressed approval of his *Economist* articles 'so far at least as the theoretical statement does'.[43]

It remains to be seen, if and to what extent, this admiration for Cairnes's *Economist* articles was to influence Mill when he came to write in 1868 one of the most controversial of all his works, the pamphlet *England and Ireland*.[44] In this pamphlet Mill abandoned his previously ambivalent views on Irish land in dramatic fashion, arguing unequivocally, on political and economic grounds, for fixity of tenure in Ireland. As E. D. Steele has commented, 'for the first time in all Mill had written and said about Irish land' he appealed 'to the notions of property in land cherished by the peasantry, which were quite different from those embodied in the laws of the United Kingdom'.[45] Mill conceded that absolute ownership of land by landlords in Britain had not proved unacceptable to the people. This was not so in Ireland. According to Steele, 'English landlords were now really apprehensive that a surrender to fundamental principles in Ireland would really encourage the radical wing of the Liberal party and its working-class allies to exploit it against themselves'.[46] Here clearly was a principle, as Lord Kimberly remarked on another occasion, 'which might easily cross the channel'.[47]

The hostile reception which greeted the publication of *England and Ireland* centred on its alleged attack on private property in land. Lord Bessborough saw Mill as a Fenian with 'plundering views'.[48] The *Times* wrote of 'this sweeping interference with the rights of property'. Every man, advised the *Times*, 'should make up his mind whether the received laws of property are to be upheld in the United Kingdom; or whether, beginning first with Ireland, we are to establish principles which would unsettle our whole social fabric . . . the first thing to be borne in mind is that every theory accepted for Ireland is accepted in England also'.[49] Mill was variously seen as a communist, a Fenian, a disciple of Proudhon or even of Jack Cade. In the subsequent House of Commons debate, Mill's pamphlet figures prominently and was attacked for undermining property rights. What heresy, you may well ask, did the proverbially moderate Mill preach in *England and Ireland* to draw such odium upon his head?

J. E. Cairnes, J. S. Mill and Ireland

In *England and Ireland*, Mill declared that the right of the labourer to appropriate the fruits of his toil was the 'foundation of property in land'. Before the Conquest, wrote Mill, 'the Irish people knew nothing of absolute property in land'. The idea of property in land in the Irish mind was connected with the right of the cultivator, not that of the rent-receiver. England forced on Ireland 'her own idea of absolute property in land'.[50]

Mill saw English laws and usages, especially with regard to land, as inappropriate to Ireland. As far as he was concerned, 'heroic remedies' were again to be prescribed for Ireland. Speaking in the House of Commons on the Maguire motion, Mill stated that in relation to Ireland 'there is a strong presumption that the remedy must be much stronger and more drastic than any that has yet been applied', for 'great and obstinate evils require great remedies'.[51] Such changes might be 'revolutionary' he declared, but 'revolutionary measures are the thing now required. It is not necessarily that the revolution should be violent, still less that it should be unjust.' No scruple of 'purely English birth', he argued, 'ought to stay our hands from affecting, since it has come to that, a real revolution in the economical and social conditions of Ireland'. For Mill, 'the rule of Ireland' now rightfully belongs 'to those who, by means consistent with justice would 'make the cultivators of the soil of Ireland the owners of it'. To support his stand, Mill drew on the experience of India to provide evidence for the Gladstonian notion that Ireland should be governed by Irish ideas. For Mill, the rule of India now devolved on men 'who passed their lives in India, and made Indian interests their professional occupation'. Such persons, he stated, needed to be stripped of their 'preconceived English ideas'. However imperfectly, argued Mill, 'India was now governed with a full perception and recognition of the differences from England. . . . What had been done for India has now to be done for Ireland'. Mill argued for the establishment of a Commission that would examine every farm that was let to a tenant, with the objective of replacing the existing variable with fixed rents. Mill saw these measures as necessary, since he felt that the time had passed for a more 'amicable mediation' of the State between the landlord and the tenant. There must, he argued, be 'compulsory powers' and a 'strong judicial inquiry'. This annual rent would be either guaranteed by or paid directly by the State to the landlord.[52] As R. D. C. Black has commented, 'the most important feature [of *England and Ireland*] . . . and the one which most startled and antagonised the upholders of the "rights of property" was the suggestion that rents should be controlled by law and not determined by market forces'. This should not have come as any great surprise for, as Professor Black observed, this proposal had been put forward by Cairnes in his *Economist* articles of 1865.[53]

Clearly the parallels between the *Economist* articles and Mill's *England and Ireland* are extremely impressive. Cairnes's radical shift of position with respect to (i) his critique of the absolute ownership of land by landlords which resulted in his doctrine of qualified rights of landowners, (ii) his critique of the transfer of English models of economic and social organisation, and of their appropriateness to Irish conditions, and (iii) his rejection of competition and contract in favour of greater State supervision and control, are all systematically reproduced in Mill's *England and Ireland*. Given Mill's enthusiastic approval of these articles when they were written, it is hardly coincidental that Mill should have been profoundly influenced by their contents. We would suggest that in attempting to explain Mill's radical deviations in *England and Ireland*, a major, if not the major influence, must be sought in the writings of Cairnes, especially in the *Economist* articles.

By way of concluding this section of the paper, it should be pointed out that Cairnes returned to this topic when, in 1869, John Morley, the editor of the *Fortnightly Review*, requested him to submit a paper on the subject.[54] This resulted in 'Political economy and land' which was published in 1870.[55] Here he examined again the basis of property in land. He reiterated his doctrine of the qualified rights of ownership along with his arguments for state intervention in dealing with land. Cairnes argued that only a political economy which was committed to *laissez-faire* could oppose such State intervention. Henry Maine wrote a critical review of this paper in the *Pall Mall Gazette* in which he declared that investigations into the 'true foundations of property' were 'speculatively idle' and 'practically dangerous'.[56] Mill in contrast commented that he had 'never seen the ethical distinction between property in land and in moveables so thoroughly and clearly worked out, and the philosophical limits both of the property doctrine and of the counter-doctrine so well stated'.[57]

In his first thoughts on Ireland, Cairnes rejected 'heroic remedies'. The drastic measures usually associated with Mill's *England and Ireland* (1868) were first canvassed much earlier in the pages of the *Economist* in 1865 by John Elliot Cairnes. Cairnes reiterated these radical views elsewhere. Writing to his friend Leonard Courtney on 6 April 1866, Cairnes declared that he was 'delighted to find that your opinions on the land question are "revolutionary" and "socialistic"'. And on 27 August 1869, he told Courtney that with reference to Irish land, 'my ideas on the subject are becoming every day more revolutionary'. By 'revolutionary', he meant 'upsetting radically existing notions respecting landed property'.[58] Clearly Cairnes's relationship with Mill was not as 'deferential' as E. D. Steele claims it to have been,[59] while Cairnes as an exponent of 'rigid individualism' and as a timid epigone of Mill, in Willard Wolfe's estimation, is a gross caricature.[60]

III

We have been concerned in the previous section with highlighting the importance of just one aspect of the writings of J. E. Cairnes, and on the basis of this examination it is difficult to sustain the view of Cairnes as merely an acolyte to Mill. Cairnes had a real, if limited, influence on the sixth edition of Mill's *Principles of political economy;* but his pioneering articles in the *Economist* anticipated by a number of years, more systematically and with more cogent argumentation, the most controversial aspects of Mill's pamphlet *England and Ireland*. In passing, one might note, that there was by no means complete unanimity between Mill and Cairnes in matters of economic theory. There were, for instance, important differences between them concerning the theory of interest, supply and demand, and costs of production.

Cairnes's reputation as the Abdiel of orthodoxy seems to be based largely on his continued defence of the wages-fund theory when Mill had already recanted it. The shadow of Mill, under which Cairnes wrote, has arguably all but obscured his contributions to several other areas of economic thought. In general, Cairnes's reputation rests largely on his two major works within the mainstream of economic analysis, respectively his first and last works, *The character and logical method of political economy* (1857, 2nd edition, expanded 1875), and *Some leading principles of political economy* (1874). In particular, his *Leading principles* is seen as the final restatement of classical political economy in the Ricardo-Mill tradition. It is interesting to note, in spite of the impeccably orthodox credentials of the *Leading principles*, that, according to Kaldor among others, the theory of 'excess capacity', which was outlined in Sraffa's famous article in the *Economic Journal* in 1926, is to be found 'in essentials' in Cairnes's last work.[61]

Cairnes's *Character and logical method of political economy*, according to Professor R. D. C. Black, 'stands as the definitive statement of the methodology of the English classical school'.[62] Such a work, wrote the historian H. T. Buckle to Cairnes, 'augurs well for the University of Dublin'.[63] Walter Bagehot, in his obituary of Cairnes in the *Economist* in 1875, wrote that in this work Cairnes 'defines better, as we think, than any previous writer, the exact sort of science, which political economy is, the kind of reasoning which it uses and the nature of the relation which it, as an abstract science, bears to the concrete world'.[64] His substantial writings on Bastiat, Comte, and Herbert Spencer are best seen as contributions to this aspect of political economy.[65] Despite Cairnes's undoubted theoretical ability, and his commitment to a rigorous deductivist methodology, he was much preoccupied by the application of economic principles to practical economic and social problems, which is reflected in many of his writings collected in his *Essays in political economy, theoretical and applied* and *Political essays*, both published in 1873.

Cairnes's writings on the gold question[66] have been described as 'among the most important works of the nineteenth century on monetary theory'.[67] His *Examination into the principles of currency involved in the Bank Charter Act of 1844*, published in 1854, and which was one of his earliest technical writings in political economy, was highly thought of by Thomas Tooke.[68] Jevons recognised that Cairnes's writings on gold both anticipated and corroborated his own later statistical work on this topic.[69] But the most influential of all of Cairnes's works was *The slave power*, published in 1862 when he was Professor of Jurisprudence and Political Economy in Queen's College Galway, but the substance of which formed the subject-matter of a course of lectures in Trinity College Dublin, a year or so previously.[70] This work was described by Leslie Stephen as 'the most powerful defence of the cause of the Northern States' in the American Civil War 'ever written', and which 'made a great impression both in England and America'.[71] Darwin was very impressed by *The slave power*[72] and Jevons saw it as a 'nearly or quite irrefragable piece of reasoning'.[73] It exerted, wrote Henry Fawcett 'a powerful influence on English public opinion in favour of the North' in the American Civil War.[74] Its 'practical object' was 'completely accomplished' wrote Cliffe Leslie, but its 'philosophic purpose' gave it 'a permanent value as an economic classic'.[75] The ambitious 'philosophic purpose' of *The slave power* was 'to show that the course of history is largely determined by the action of economic causes'.[76] It is scarcely surprising that Marx should show an interest in this work, and it is not widely known that Marx's own analysis of the slave economy is very much indebted to Cairnes. Indeed Cairnes remains a *bête noire* of some American economic historians, particularly Fogel and Engerman in their controversial revisionist study of American slavery, *Time on the Cross*, where Cairnes is condemned as an originator of a pre-cliometric, unreconstructed understanding of slavery.[77] Engerman writes that Marx drew largely on Cairnes in his analysis of the slave South, as indeed did subsequent Marxist scholars.[78] This remains true to this day — Eugene Genovese, perhaps the leading contemporary Marxist writer on slavery, is very much indebted to the work of John Elliot Cairnes.[79] Maurice Dobb, the late Marxist economist at Cambridge, claimed that Cairnes's analysis of a slave economy could be a fruitful model for an understanding of the economics of imperialism.[80]

But it is in the area of economic policy that Cairnes deserves least his reputation for unimpeachable orthodoxy. This is an aspect of his work we would like to pursue, particularly in relation to his writings on *laissez-faire*. Of interest here is the extent to which his position on *laissez-faire* arose from his writings on Ireland. In his book, *The end of laissez-faire*, published in 1926, J. M. Keynes (whose father John Neville Keynes wrote the extensive entry on Cairnes in Palgrave's *Dictionary of political economy*) stated that Cairnes 'was perhaps the first orthodox economist to deliver a frontal attack upon *laissez-faire* in general'.[81] This was in a lecture 'Political economy and *laissez-faire*' which he delivered at University College London in 1870. *Laissez-faire*, he argued, had 'no scientific basis whatsoever' and was 'at best a mere handy rule of practice'.[82] As R. D. C. Black has put it, 'already in 1870 Cairnes had exploded the myth that economists were inevitably committed to approval of the policy of *laissez-faire*'.[83] Or as H. D. Marshall has stated, 'if Mill can be described as one who, despite his sympathy for social reform, still clung to the concept of individualism and *laissez-faire*, Cairnes may best be described as one who never had any doubts about the undesirability of opposing any proposal for interfering with the free operation of the market'.[84] Indeed Cairnes's mordant critique of Bastiat is probably best seen within the context of the whole *laissez-faire* debate. He attacked Bastiat's doctrine of the harmony of interests, which for Bastiat was a quasi-theological belief which provided him with an invulnerable metaphysical underpinning for the economic policy of *laissez-faire*.[85] It was for this reason that Veblen commended Cairnes for making the foundations of economics more scientific, though he realised that the opportunity cost of this increased scientificity was a concomitant decrease in metaphysical charm. It was, in Veblen's view, a tribute to Cairnes that, in his hand, political economy had become an even more dismal science than even Carlyle had imagined.[86] P. T. Homan succinctly summarised Cairnes's position when he stated that he undermined the adequacy of the classical system 'as a basis for the political precept of *laissez-faire*' by 'divorcing the system from a beneficient order of nature and by emphasising the "hypothetical nature of its laws"'.[87]

It is, to coin a phrase, no accident that the 'first frontal attack' on *laissez-faire* should come out of the Irish experience. Cairnes rejected the view that the contract between landlords and tenants, particularly in Ireland, was an ordinary commercial transaction. In Great Britain land was but one among many modes of profitable investment, but this was not so in Ireland.[88] Lacking a significant industrial sector, the large Irish population created an intense demand for a fixed supply of land. Cairnes characterised competition for land in Ireland as that 'of impoverished men, bidding under the pressure of prospective exile or beggary'.[89] Cairnes, in 1866, saw the Landed Estates Court as 'proceeding according to rules known to our existing system of jurisprudence; it set aside solemn contracts',[90] a course he very much approved of. As Oliver McDonagh put it, Cairnes 'first argued for peasant proprietorship upon the ground that property in land was not absolute but qualified, and subject to the labourer's right to a share of the fruits of his work'.[91] McDonagh is here, of course, referring to Cairnes's *Economist* articles, as is Joseph Lee when he stated that 'Cairnes startled public opinion in 1865 by advocating peasant proprietorship in Ireland'.[92] John Bright, writing to Gladstone on 15 October 1869, confessed that Cairnes's proposal to introduce fixed rents 'alarmed him a good deal'.[93]

In a further letter to Gladstone on 1 January, 1870, Bright 'recoiled at a particular manifestation of the new British radicalism'[94] — this was Cairnes's article 'Political economy and land' in the *Fortnightly Review* of January, 1870, where Cairnes, among other things, advocated State control of rents.[95] It must be noted that even before Cairnes began informing Mill on Irish affairs, Ireland had presented problems for Mill, particularly in relation to property in land. A later economist, J. Shield Nicholson, opposing Mill's analysis, made the observation that 'no doubt Mill's views were influenced by the condition of Ireland when he wrote, and by its history' and proceeded to admonish Mill for arguing from 'a particular case'.[96]

But the issue of Ireland as a 'particular case' must be viewed in the context of the debate concerning the applicability of political economy to Ireland. In the mid-nineteenth century a number of authors pointed out that the English agricultural model was not appropriate to Ireland. As Henry Dix Hutton put it 'English land tenure ... does not furnish a universal standard. There is no country to which English tenure, considered as an absolute test, is less applicable than Ireland'.[97] And as Mill claimed in *England and Ireland* and in his contributions to the debates on Fortescue's Land Bill (1866) and Maguire's motion (1868), Irish problems were not to be solved by a political economy based on English experience and ideas.[98] Indeed there was a widespread view in Ireland that the writs of political economy did not run in this country. The laws of political economy were, no doubt, universal, but they did not, however, apply to Ireland. Professor Bastable, who succeeded Cairnes both at Galway and Trinity College Dublin, later in the century, felt it necessary to rebut the heresy that 'economic principles are not applicable to Ireland'.[99] Hancock entitled one of his publications, produced significantly in 1847, *Three lectures on the question: Should the principles of political economy be disregarded at the present crisis?*[100] Hancock saw quite early, that 'the orthodox doctrines of political economy if applied rigidly in Ireland' led to 'startling results'.[101] John Bright suspected, doubtless in exasperation, that political economy was 'a science unknown ... in Ireland'.[102] The 'Limerick declaration' of 1868, a manifesto by an assembly of Roman Catholic priests in favour of repeal, announced, no doubt as a cogent reason for severing the connection with England, that 'Ireland had had enough of political economy'.[103] As Black notes, 'To them, and to most Irishmen ... political economy meant *laissez-faire* and freedom of contract, not the doctrines of Mill and Cairnes'.[104]

While the applicability of political economy to Ireland was vigorously attacked, this did not imply a lack of interest in political economy in Ireland. Mill's views were well known in Ireland — his *England and Ireland* was popular here,[105] and extracts from his *Principles* relating to Ireland, together with his Parliamentary speeches on Fortescue's Bill and Maguire's motion were published in Ireland, 'not by me', as he recounts in his *Autobiography*, 'but with my permission'.[106] Cairnes, in his lecture 'Political economy and *laissez-faire*' stated that 'in the not very flourishing town of Galway' the degree of interest taken in economic science is many times, perhaps five or six times greater than in London, basing his view on the comparative number of students of political economy in Galway and London![107] Even in Tuam itself, according to the economist W. E. Hearn, 'under the gloomy shadow of St. Jarlath's — long the undisputed kingdom of Old Night', the 'faith and morals' of the townspeople were to be 'contaminated by a course of lectures in very heretical political economy'.[108]

In Ireland, according to an article in the *Irish Tribune* in July 1848, entitled 'The rights of labour', unsigned but sometimes erroneously attributed to James Fintan Lalor, what was bad in political economy 'has been acted upon, but the good has been totally neglected'. Political economy would not do too much damage, according to the author, if it were confined to 'turnip-headed candidates' for political office who uttered words like 'capital', sounds 'devoid of meaning to them'. The author, however, did not think much of Whately. 'But there are others', he fulminated 'whose poison is more insidious, and who have taken the best means of diffusing it through our veins — such as one Whately, a goodly specimen of the foreign vermin we have allowed to crawl over us — of such we must beware'.[109] It is a rather nice irony that it was another Irishman, from Trinity College Dublin, John Kells Ingram, who did not fear to speak in defence of the scientific status of political economy when it was impugned by Sir Francis Galton at a meeting of the British Association in 1877.[110]

Coming out of Ireland, it is little wonder that Cairnes should have become sceptical of the universality of the laws of political economy, of the alleged beneficent order of nature, of the theory of the harmony of interests, and of the sacredness of landed property. One feature, according to Cairnes, which was 'noticeable as more or less prominently characterising' all schemes 'recently offered [around 1870] to public notice for the settlement of the Irish land question' was 'a profound distrust of Political Economy'. Just in proportion he added, 'as a plan gives promise of being effective, does the author feel it necessary to assume an attitude, if not of hostility, then of apology, towards the science. It is either sneered at as unpractical and perverse, or its authority is respectfully put aside as of no account in a country so exceptionally situated as Ireland'.[111] For Cairnes a political economy the 'sum and substance' of whose teaching was the maxim *'laissez-faire'* had no relevance to Irish problems. In the discussions about the 1870 Irish Land Bill, Cairnes wrote that 'political economy was again and again appealed

J. E. Cairnes, J. S. Mill and Ireland

to as having pronounced against that measure' because the Bill 'interfered with freedom of contract, violated the rule of *laissez-faire*', charges, Cairnes added, which were 'perfectly true, and which would have been decisive against the Bill had these phrases really possessed the scientific authority which members of parliament supposed them to possess'.[112]

We hope we have made a *prima facie* case for a revaluation of Cairnes's status as a political economist. We noted the rapid change in his thinking on Ireland, from rejecting 'heroic remedies' to embracing what he called 'revolutionary' and 'socialistic' doctrines with respect to private property in land. He made some contributions to Mill's thinking on Ireland in the sixth edition of the *Principles*, but his greatest influence, heretofore uninvestigated, was that of his *Economist* articles on Mill's most controversial work *England and Ireland*. In more general terms, Cairnes had a profound impact on Mill's increasing hostility to *laissez-faire* economics. We suggested that Cairnes's reputation for unsullied orthodoxy is based on his last-ditch defence of the wages-fund theory. This, we argued, does a serious injustice to his important contributions to several areas in economic analysis and policy. Finally, we attempted to explain the genesis of a number of Cairnes's contributions to political economy by locating them in their Irish context. Using Cairnes as a basis we then broadened the discussion to consider, tentatively, the uneasy relationship perceived to have existed in the nineteenth century between Ireland and political economy. And, finally, we noted the mischief wrought by Ireland, with its infuriatingly different socio-economic arrangements and ideas, to that quintessentially English discourse — political economy.

Notes

1. [J. S. Mill] review of J. E. Cairnes, *The slave power* (London, 1862), in *Westminster Review*, n.s. 22 (1862), 489-90.

2. See entry in *Dictionary of national biography; Palgrave's dictionary of political economy* (London, 1874); R. D. C. Black, *The statistical and social inquiry society of Ireland: centenary volume 1847-1947* (Dublin, 1947); Adelaide Weinberg, *John Elliot Cairnes and the American Civil War,* (London, 1967), pp 10-18.

3. Cairnes to Nesbitt. 9 May 1859 (London School of Economics, Mill-Taylor Collection, Vol. XLIV, item 23).

4. F. E. Mineka and D. N. Lindley, eds., *The later letters of John Stuart Mill,* in *Collected works,* XIV (Toronto, 1972), p. xxxviii.

5. *Ibid.*

6. *Ibid.*, Vol. XV, p. 975, reproduced in J. S. Mill, *Principles of political economy*, ed., J. M. Robson, in *CW III* (Toronto, 1965), Appendix H, p. 1072.

7. 'Ireland', *Edinburgh Review*, 119 (1864). pp 279-304.

8. Mill to Cairnes, 28 March 1864, *CW*, Vol. XV, pp 929-30, No. 684.

9. Mill to Cairnes, 3 October 1864, *CW*, Vol. XV, pp 957-59, No. 721.

10. J. S. Mill, *Principles of political economy* (5th ed., London 1862), Vol. 1, p. 407.

11. *Ibid.*, Vol. 1, p. 407.

12. Cairnes to Mill, 13 October 1864 (L. S. E., M-T Coll., Vol. LVI (i) (A), item 16).

13. Mill to Cairnes, 1 Dec. 1864, *CW*, Vol. XV, pp 967-69, No. 728.

14. Cairnes to Mill, 6 December 1864 (L. S. E., M-T Coll., Vol. LVI (i) A, item 18), mostly reproduced in Appendix H, pp 1056-57.

15. Mill to Cairnes, 12 December 1864, *CW*, Vol. XV, pp 975-79, No. 734, reproduced in part in Appendix H, pp 1072-73.

16. Cairnes's *Notes* have been reproduced *in toto* in Appendix H, pp 1075-86.

17. J. S. Mill, *Principles of political economy* (6th ed., London, 1865), Vol. 1, pp 412-14.

18. Appendix H, pp 1075-76.

19. *Ibid.*, p. 1076.

20. *Ibid.*, p. 1076.

21. *Ibid.*, p. 1076.

22. *Ibid.*, p. 1076.

23. *Ibid.*, p. 1077.

24. *Ibid.*, p. 1078.

25. *Ibid.*, pp 1079-80.

26. *Ibid.*, p. 1080.

27. *Ibid.*, p. 1081.

28. *Ibid.*, pp 1081-82.

29. J. S. Mill, *Principles of political economy* (6th ed., London, 1865), Vol. 1, pp 416-18, and Appendix H, p. 1082.

30. Appendix H, pp 1082-83.

31. Mill to Cairnes, 5 Jan. 1865, *CW*, Vol. XVI, pp 985-87, No. 741, and Appendix H, p. 1088.

32. J. S. Mill, *Principles of political economy* (6th ed., London, 1865), Vol. 1, pp 416-18.

33. Cairnes to Mill, 24 January 1865 (L.S.E., M-T Coll., Vol. LVI (i) A, item 22).

34. Cairnes to Eliza Cairnes, 9 May 1865 (National Library of Ireland, Cairnes Papers, MS 8940 (II)).

35. *Ibid.*, 23 May 1865.

36. D. C. Heron, 'Historical statistics of Ireland', *Journal of the Dublin Statistical Society*, Vol. II, 1862, pp 235-57; M. Longfield, Presidential address *JDSS*, Vol. IV, 1865, pp 129-54; J. K. Ingram, 'Consideration on the state of Ireland', *JDSS*, Vol. IV, 1864, pp 13-26; W. N. Hancock, *Report of the supposed progressive decline of Irish prosperity* (Dublin, 1863).

37. *Economist*, 14 October 1865, p. 1238.

38. *Economist*, 21 October 1865, p. 1269.

39. *Economist*, 14 October 1865, p. 1238.

40. *Economist*, 12 May 1866, p. 559.

41. Cairnes to Mill, 20 May 1867 (L.S.E., M-T Coll., Vol. LVI (i) A, item 43).

42. Mill to Cairnes, 6 January 1866, *CW*, Vol. XVI, p. 1134, No. 904.

43. Cairnes to Mill, 9 January 1866 (L.S.E., M-T Coll., Vol. LVI (i) A, item 32).

44. John Stuart Mill, *England and Ireland* (London, 1868). Reprinted in *CW* (Toronto, 1982), Vol. VI, pp 507-532.

J. E. Cairnes, J. S. Mill and Ireland

45. E. D. Steele, 'J. S. Mill and the Irish question: reform, and the integrity of the empire, 1865-1870' in *Historical Journal*, xiii, No. 3 (1970), p. 429.

46. *Ibid.,* p. 437.

47. Cited in E. D. Steele, *Irish land and British politics: tenant right and nationality 1865-1870* (Cambridge, 1974), p. 293.

48. Cited in Steele, 'J. S. Mill and the Irish Question: reform, and the integrity of the empire, 1865-1870', p. 438.

49. *Ibid.,* p. 439.

50. *CW,* Vol. VI, p. 513.

51. J. S. Mill *Chapters and speeches on the Irish land question* (London, 1870), p. 110.

52. *CW,* Vol. VI, p. 519.

53. R. D. C. Black, *Economic thought and the Irish question 1817-1870* (Cambridge, 1960), p. 54.

54. Cairnes to Mill, 21 December 1869 (L.S.E. M-T Coll., item 54).

55. J. E. Cairnes, 'Political economy and land', *Fortnightly Review*, n.s., 7 (1870), pp 41-43, reprinted in *Essays in political economy, theoretical and applied* (London, 1873), pp 187-231.

56. *Pall Mall Gazette,* 6 January 1870, pp 6-7.

57. Mill to Cairnes, 11 January 1870, *CW,* Vol. XVII, p. 1676, No. 1509.

58. Cairnes to Leonard Courtney, 1 Sept. 1869 (L.S.E., Courtney Collection, Vol. 1, item 58). Leonard Henry Courtney (1832-1918) succeeded Cairnes as Professor of Political Economy at University College London. He became M.P. and was later created 1st Baron Courtney of Penwith. See DNB.

59. E. D. Steele, 'J. S. Mill and the Irish question: *the principles of political economy*, 1848-1865'. *Historical Journal*, xiii, No. 2 (1970), p. 232.

60. Williard Wolfe, *From radicalism to socialism* (New Haven and London, 1975), p. 50.

61. Nicholas Kaldor, *Essays on value and distribution* (London, 1960), p. 63. See also E. H. Chamberlin, *The theory of monopolistic competition* (Cambridge, Massachusetts and London, 1956), p. 106. P. Sraffa, 'The laws of returns under competitive conditions', *Economic Journal*, xxxvi (1926), pp 535-50.

62. R. D. C. Black, 'Cairnes', *International encyclopedia of the social sciences*, Vol. 2 (1968), pp 257-58.

63. H. T. Buckle to Cairnes, 1 March 1858 (N.L.I., Cairnes Papers, MS 8944 (5)).

64. Reprinted in *Biographical Studies*, ed., R. H. Hutton, (London, 1881), p. 362.

65. J. E. Cairnes, 'Bastiat', *Fortnightly Review*, n.s. 8 (1870), pp 411-28; 'M. Comte and political economy', *Fortnightly Review*, n.s. 7 (1870), pp 579-602; 'Mr. Spencer on social evolution', *Fortnightly Review*, n.s. 17 (1875), pp 63-82, and 'Mr. Spencer on the study of sociology', *Fortnightly Review*, n.s. 17 (1875), pp 200-13.

66. J. E. Cairnes, 'The Laws, according to which a depreciation of the precious metals consequent upon an increase of supply takes place, considered in connection with the recent Gold Discoveries'. Paper read to the British Association, September 1858. Published in the *Journal of the Dublin Statistical Society*, II (1859), pp 236-69. 'Essays towards an experimental solution of the gold question', *Fraser's Magazine*, 60 (1859), pp 267-78; 'Essay towards a solution of the gold question', *Fraser's Magazine*, 61 (1860), pp 38-53; Review of M. Chevalier, *On the probable fall in the value of gold: the commercial and social consequences which may ensue, and the measures which it invites* (London, 1859), *Edinburgh Review*, 112 (1860), pp 1-33, reprinted in *Essays in political economy: theoretical and applied* (London, 1873), pp 109-165.

67. 'Cairnes', entry in *Encyclopedia Britannica* (Chicago, 1963) by T. W. Hutchinson.

68. Tooke to Cairnes, 27 March 1856 (N.L.I., Cairnes Papers, MS 8944 (4)).

69. See R. D. C. Black, 'Jevons and Cairnes', *Economica*, 27 (1960), pp 214-232.

70. J. E. Cairnes, *The slave power* (London, 1862), p. vii. A second edition followed in 1863.

117

71. See Stephen's entry on 'Cairnes' in DNB.

72. F. Darwin, ed., *The life and letters of Charles Darwin* (London, 1887), Vol. III, p. 11.

73. Quoted by R. D. C. Black, 'Jevons and Cairnes', p. 223.

74. Henry Fawcett, 'Professor Cairnes', *Fortnightly Review*, n.s. 18 (1875), p. 152.

75. T. E. Cliffe Leslie, 'Professor Cairnes', *Essays in political economy*, 2nd edition (Dublin and London, 1888), p. 61. Originally an obituary in the *Academy*, 17 July 1875.

76. *The slave power*, p. vii.

77. See R. W. Fogel and S. L. Engermann, *Time on the Cross: The economics of American negro slavery* (Boston and Toronto, 1974).

78. S. L. Engermann, 'Marxist economic studies of the slave south', *Marxist Perspectives*, 1 (1978), p. 149.

79. See E. Genovese, *Political economy of slavery: studies in economy and society of the slave south* (New York, 1967); see also Charles Post 'The American road to capitalism', *New Left Review*, No. 133, May-June, 1982, pp 33-34.

80. Maurice Dobb, *Political economy and capitalism* (London, 1964), p. 251.

81. J. M. Keynes, *The end of laissez-faire* (London, 1926), p. 26.

82. Published in *Fortnightly Review*, 10 (1871), pp 80-97. The quotation is from p. 86.

83. Black, *Centenary volume*, p. 52.

84. H. D. Marshall, *The great economists: a history of economic thought* (New York, 1967), p. 126.

85. See Cairnes, 'Bastiat', pp 411-28.

86. Thorstein Veblen, 'Why is economics not an evolutionary science?', *The Quarterly Journal of Economics*, xii (1898), pp 385-86.

87. P. T. Homan, cited by H. D. Marshall, p. 102.

88. J. E. Cairnes, *Political essays* (London, 1873), p. 160.

89. *Ibid.*, p. 161.

90. *Ibid.*, p. 173.

91. Oliver McDonagh, *Ireland* (Englewood Cliffs, 1968), p. 37.

92. Joseph Lee, *The modernisation of Irish society 1848-1918* (Dublin, 1973), p. 26.

93. Bright to Gladstone (B.M. Add MSS 44112), quoted in Black, *Economic thought and the Irish question*, p. 58.

94. Steele, *Irish land and British politics*, p. 293.

95. *Fortnightly Review*, 7 (1870), pp 41-63.

96. J. Shield Nicholson, *Elements of political economy* (2nd ed., London, 1909), p. 113.

97. Henry Dix Hutton, *Transactions of the National Association for the Promotion of Social Science* (London, 1868), quoted by Black, *Economic thought and the Irish question*, p. 57.

98. See above pp 13-14.

99. C. F. Bastable, *An examination of some current objections to the study of political economy* (Dublin, 1884), pp 20, 5.

100. Dublin, 1847.

101. W. H. Dodd, K.C., in *Belfast Literary Society, 1801-1901; historical sketch with memoirs of some distinguished members* (Belfast, 1902), pp 106-7, quoted in Black, *Centenary volume*, p. 58.

102. Bright to Gladstone, 15 October 1869 (B.M., Add. MSS 44112), quoted in Black, *Economic thought and the Irish question*, p. 58.

103. Quoted in Black, *Economic thought and the Irish question*, p. 70.

104. *Ibid.*, p. 71.

105. J. S. Mill, *Autobiography* (New York, 1964), p. 205.

106. *Ibid.*, p. 206. See also Mill to Cairnes, 16 November 1869, *CW*, Vol. XVII, pp 1663-66, No. 1423. The volume in question is *Chapters and speeches on the Irish land question* (London, 1870).

J. E. Cairnes, J. S. Mill and Ireland

107. 'Political economy and *laissez-faire*', *Fortnightly Review*, n.s. 10 (1871), p. 81.

108. W. E. Hearn, *Prize essay on the remedies of Irish distress* (London, 1851), pp 118-19.

109. 'The rights of labour', *Irish Tribune*, July 1848. We are indebted to Ms. R. O'Neill of University College Galway for providing us with this reference. We are informed by Professor T. P. O'Neill of University College Galway that the probable author of this article is Thomas Devin Reilly.

110. J. K. Ingram, 'The present position and prospects of political economy', addressed to section F of the British Association, 1878. Published in the *Journal of the Dublin Statistical Society*, VII (1876-79), Appendix.

111. 'Political economy and land', p. 41.

112. 'Political economy and *laissez-faire*', p. 90.

0314
0321
0322

120-37

Longfield, Mountifort

The Irish dissenters and nineteenth-century political economy

by R. D. Collison Black

I

To be a dissenter, according to the dictionaries, is to refuse to accept established doctrine; which implies in turn the existence of an orthodoxy of some sort.

According to the view of the history of economic ideas which prevailed some forty years ago, such an orthodoxy had indeed existed in political economy throughout the first seventy years of the nineteenth century. Its sources and character were well known and could be briefly summed up. It derived initially from Adam Smith's *Wealth of nations,* had absorbed as one of its essentials the doctrine of Malthus's *Essay on population,* received its definitive theoretical statement in Ricardo's *Principles of political economy* and had been finally rounded out and re-stated by John Stuart Mill in his *Principles* in 1848 — a re-statement which remained unchallenged until the appearance of Jevons's *Theory of political economy* in 1871.

The core of the classical orthodoxy which had been built up in this way was a cost of production theory of value, in which labour was seen as the major element of real cost and as in some sense the 'best' measure of value. Only Ricardo had sought (vainly) to establish an invariable measure of value and to make labour the sole source of value.

This cost theory of value in turn formed the foundation for a theory of production and distribution dominated by the law of diminishing returns and the Malthusian theory of population. In this the 'Ricardian' theory of rent was the best known and best regarded feature; the wage fund theory and the complementary theory of profits as a return (falling through time) mainly on circulating capital tended to be treated as crude aberrations long superseded by the superior techniques of neo-classical price theory.[1]

That nineteenth century economic literature encompassed a far greater variety and richness than is conveyed in this stereotype began to be recognised after the publication of Seligman's famous articles 'On some neglected British economists'.[2] It was not until

120

The Irish dissenters

some thirty years later that detailed research results began to be published on the work of the many authors to whom Seligman had first drawn attention; notable among these was Professor Marian Bowley's *Nassau Senior and classical economics* which put forward what was to become an influential view, that the economists of the first half of the nineteenth century could in fact be divided into four groups — 'the French school, particularly Say and his immediate followers; the Ricardians; the group which we may call the English dissenters, which includes economists as far apart in time as Lauderdale and Macleod, and the German theorists from Hufeland to von Mangoldt'.[3]

While naturally giving most attention to the work of Senior, Professor Bowley included among the [English!] Dissenters both Mountifort Longfield and Isaac Butt, the first and second holders of the Whately Professorship. Her suggestion that 'in Ireland . . . Longfield bid fair to set up a distinctive school of economists'[4] was one which I followed up in an article published in 1945,[5] contending that Longfield did really found such a local school, which included not only Butt but other early occupants of the Whately chair such as J. A. Lawson and W. Neilson Hancock. These then were the first group of Irish dissenters who in Schumpeter's 'Review of the Troops'[6] were ranked not with the Ricardians, but with 'The Men who wrote above their Time'.

Such was what one might call the topography of the relationship between the Irish Dissenters and mainstream English classical political economy as it had been mapped out when Schumpeter wrote. However Mark Blaug's well-known comment remains true — 'there is a mutual interaction between past and present economic thinking for, whether we set it down in so many words or not the history of economic thought is being rewritten every generation'.[7] The history of economic thought has indeed been re-written several times since Schumpeter, and in different versions the place of the early Whately professors, as dissenters or otherwise has been variously re-assessed. It is these re-assessments and their validity or otherwise that I wish mainly to discuss here.

II

The first major re-assessment of classical economic thought after that given in Schumpeter's *History of economic analysis* came with the appearance in 1951 of the first volume of Sraffa's superb edition of *The works and correspondence of David Ricardo*. It would be fair to say that the interpretation of Ricardo's system which Sraffa gave in his introduction to the first volume of the edition, the *Principles of political economy and taxation,* came to dominate thinking on that subject for the ensuing thirty years. Indeed it is in one of the most recent works on Ricardian theory that one of the most concise statements of the interpretation of that theory which Sraffa promoted is to be found:—

Ricardo's thesis of the long-run tendency of the economy towards a stationary state situation is based on a set of crucial assumptions — diminishing returns in agriculture, reinvestment of profits and a theory of distribution in which the income of the capitalist class represents a residual. This set of assumptions implies a strict connection between the rate of profit and the rate of capital accumulation. It is thus necessary, for a theory which aims at proving the validity of that thesis, to solve the problem of the unambiguous determination of the profit rate and to show how diminishing returns affect its behaviour through time. These problems found a straightforward solution within Ricardo's primitive agricultural model of the *Essay on Profits.* [1815] It was in the attempt to escape the limitations of this model that Ricardo felt, in the *Principles* the need for a developed theory of value.[8]

Ricardo's convoluted thinking on labour as the measure and source of value was thus displayed in a new and much more sympathetic light by Sraffa's argument that it was crucial for the Ricardian analysis of distribution to 'find a measure of value which would be invariant to changes in the division of the product; for if a rise or fall of wages by itself brought about a change in the magnitude of the social product, it would be hard to determine accurately the effect on profits'.[9]

It was out of this Sraffa interpretation of Ricardo that there developed the view that 'there were, broadly speaking, two quite distinct and rival traditions in nineteenth-century economic thought as to the order and mode of determination of phenomena of exchange and income distribution'.[10]

One of these deriving from Adam Smith treated the value of any commodity as being determined as the sum of the various expenses or costs involved in its production; these expenses depending upon the necessary payments for land, capital and labour and upon the various amounts of these needed to produce the commodity in question. Determination of these necessary payments was viewed in a general supply-and-demand framework . . .

This line of thought is seen as running from Smith through Malthus to 'the Senior-Longfield group' and so on to John Stuart Mill and ultimately Marshall.

The Irish dissenters

The second main line of tradition also derived from Smith, even if in a quasi-Hegelian manner from certain doctrines or propositions of Smith inverted (and hence transmuted) by Ricardo. First, Smith's peculiar theory of value . . . was refashioned by Ricardo so as to make conditions of production, and in particular quantities of labour expended in production, the basic determinant alike in capitalist and pre-capitalist society. In doing so he rejected the Adding-up-components Theory, and by implication rejected the possibility of treating the sphere of exchange relations as an 'isolated system', and anchored the explanations of these exchange-relations firmly in conditions and circumstances of production. Secondly, whatever his reason may have been for regarding distribution as the central problem, his instinct in doing so was undoubtedly right, and his mode of treating distribution was crucial. He saw this had to be explained in terms peculiar to itself and not as an outcome of general supply-demand exchange-relations, as Smith had treated it.[11]

According to this view J. S. Mill was not, whatever he himself may have said, a developer of the Ricardian tradition. That development was the work of Marx; thereafter it lived on only in the underworld of heresies, not to re-emerge finally and fully until the publication in 1960 of Sraffa's *Production of commodities by commodities* and the subsequent growth of 'neo-Ricardian' theory.

This 'two traditions' view of the history of economic thought has never won general acceptance, even among those who were ready to agree with Sraffa's interpretation of the Ricardian 'corn model'. Most such commentators would nevertheless have drawn a very clear distinction between what Baumol once termed 'the magnificent dynamics' of the classical school and the equilibrium theories of the neo-classical writers.

Of recent years, however, we have seen the emergence of another interpretation of classical political economy which harks back to Marshall's view of the essential continuity of the earlier classical and the later neo-classical approaches to questions of value and distribution. According to this interpretation, whose main exponent is Professor Samuel Hollander of Toronto, 'the economics of Ricardo and J. S. Mill in fact comprises in its essentials an exchange system fully consistent with the marginalist elaborations. In particular, their cost-price analysis is pre-eminently an analysis of the allocation of scarce resources, proceeding in terms of general equilibrium with allowance for final demand, and the interdependence of factor and commodity markets. . . . The demand side, the functional relation between cost and output, and the supply and demand determination of wages and profits, far from being "radical departures" from

123

Ricardianism, are central to that doctrine without which neither the cost theory of price nor the inverse wage-profit relation can be understood'.[12]

I am not called upon here to discuss the merits of these two contrasting approaches to the assessment of Ricardo and to the writing of the subsequent history of classical and neo-classical economic thought,[13] but only to deal with the re-assessments of the place of the Irish dissenting economists in that history which result from them. In each case that re-assessment is substantial, and substantially different.

III

To begin with the Sraffa approach, under this the notion of dissent from Ricardian ideas is preserved, but for very different reasons from those given by Schumpeter. From being among 'the men who wrote above their time' writers like Longfield are demoted (along with Senior) to form part of 'the reaction against Ricardo' by Maurice Dobb who, having assisted Sraffa in editing Ricardo's *Works and correspondence*, may be taken as perhaps the most authoritative expositor of this approach.[14] According to Dobb, Longfield's 'concern if not preoccupation, with the emerging "Labour question" is clear' from the form of his analysis of wages and profits. Having given rather more prominence to some of the rather naively sanctimonious corollaries which Longfield (perhaps for the benefit of Archbishop Whately) drew from this than to the analysis itself, Dobb comments: 'The laws of production and distribution, apparently, are not merely made of iron but are of divine origin'.[15]

Looked at from this point of view, the dissenters become the orthodox — 'harmony theorists' defending the *status quo* or, in other words, the lackeys of the capitalists. As it had been put earlier by Ronald Meek, 'it was the *dangerous* character of Ricardo's doctrines, rather than what they believed to be their falsity, with which they were primarily concerned'.[16]

On the other hand, Dobb does credit Longfield with having developed 'a "marginal efficiency" notion of profit' and describes his treatment of intensities of demand as 'certainly a foretaste of a Jevonian Law of Diminishing Utility'. Indeed one of Dobb's comments on Longfield's *Lectures on political economy* is that 'it is evident that we have here quite a number of preliminary sketches for economic theory at the end of the century' — a comment which of course is not inconsistent with the criticisms quoted above.

The Irish dissenters

The new interpretation of Ricardo given by Hollander leads to a treatment of the work of Longfield and his followers which comes near to being the simple inverse of that given by the followers of Sraffa. From being part of the reaction against Ricardo they now appear as dedicated Ricardians — but in the process inevitably their originality as theorists of value and distribution disappears. For Hollander says of Ricardo,

While, of course, his main interests lay in long-run price determination, his economics required and, implicitly at least, hinged upon the operation of the competitive mechanism involving demand-supply analysis. His rejection of demand-supply theory did not apply to the particular version elaborated by Longfield, and Longfield himself appreciated Ricardo's objections to the 'indefinite' and 'vague' expression, 'proportion between the demand and supply' as unhelpful in the prediction of market price.[17]

Now Hollander does admit that 'there can be little doubt that Ricardo failed to appreciate the conception of marginal utility'.[18] If then, as Dobb said, Longfield gave his readers 'a foretaste of a Jevonian Law of Diminishing Utility' there would still seem to be an important difference between his treatment of price determination and that of Ricardo. However, as against this view Hollander can invoke the authority of Professor Laurence Moss who in his book on Longfield has categorized him as merely a supply-and-demand theorist, though one whose ideas of demand derived from Malthus rather than Ricardo.[19]

On the other hand Moss contends that 'Longfield's *Lectures on political economy* does contain something approximating a complete non-Ricardian theory of income distribution and not simply a series of modifications of the Ricardian analysis',[20] whereas Hollander takes the view that 'much of the discussion of the *Lectures* is unmistakably "Ricardian" . . . on the whole Longfield retained a Ricardian structure throughout'.[21]

IV

Now, the broad title given to this series of lectures is 'Economists and the Irish economy . . .' and it may be noted that these re-assessments in the history of classical economic thought raise questions with regard to both. The 'two traditions' approach, associated with the names of Sraffa and Dobb puts the Irish dissenters into the category, if not of 'hired prizefighters', certainly of harmony theorists and defenders of the *status quo*. But this must presumably refer

125

to the status quo in Ireland and hence it raises the whole issue of the attitude of the early Whately professors to conditions in Ireland generally and to the distribution of income and wealth in particular.

As against this, the 'new interpretation' of Ricardo associated mainly with the name of Hollander does more to call into question the position of the early Whately professors *as economists* — in relation to their contemporaries and their place in the history of economic ideas. It suggests that the application of the term 'dissenter' to them may be misleading, for they were not so much dissenting from the Ricardian orthodoxy as following in it and perhaps developing it to some small extent. It may be convenient to deal with this latter contention first, since it follows on somewhat more directly from my discussion of the various assessments of classical economic theory earlier in this lecture.

The question we have to deal with is essentially whether writers like Longfield were or were not Ricardians. The fact that it is possible for able and scholarly commentators such as Professors Hollander and Moss, in addition to the late Mr Dobb, to return diametrically opposite answers to this question arises from the fact that they employ different criteria to determine what constitutes the essence of a Ricardian.

For Sraffa, Dobb and their followers, as we have already seen, the key feature of the Ricardian system is that in it distribution was explained in terms peculiar to itself and not as an outcome of general supply-and-demand exchange relations. On this criterion an economist like Longfield could definitely not be classed as a Ricardian, for his analysis of distribution is characterised by statements such as 'it is evident that the wages of labour, like the exchangeable value of every thing else, must depend upon the relation between the supply and the demand'.[22] Consequently followers of the 'dual development' approach to nineteenth century economic thought must inevitably see a sharp break between Ricardo and the dissenters, just as Professor Bowley originally did although not for quite the same reasons.

On the other hand, for Hollander the essential distinguishing feature of Ricardo's work is what he calls 'the fundamental theorem on distribution' — 'the entire Ricardian scheme is designed to relate the rate of return on capital to the "value" of per capita wages (Ricardian real wages) — which in effect amounts to the proportion of the work-day devoted to the production of wages — and variations in the rate of return to (inverse) variations in the real wage rate'.[23] He contends that this theorem displays an impressive resilience in

The Irish dissenters

nineteenth century economic thought and states his 'primary conclusion that the Ricardian theorem on distribution — the inverse
wage-profit relationship — left a firm and positive impression on
the work of a number of authors normally regarded as "dissenters"
par excellence' — including Longfield.[24]

In contrast to this Moss (as Hollander himself has noted) adopts
a version of the Ricardian system 'running in terms of the agricultural model of distribution in a growth context' and treating the
role of the measure of value as basis for the inverse wage-profit
relationship as only a secondary feature of the structure.[25] Arising
from this Moss finds that 'the major area of disagreement between
Longfield and Ricardo has to do with the question of the determination of profit and wages';[26] not surprisingly he considers Longfield's marginal productivity theory of profits and productivity
theory of wages to amount to a fundamentally non-Ricardian theory
of distribution.

As between these two very different interpretations of the essence
of Ricardo, it seems to me that one focuses primarily on the structure
of Ricardian theory, the other on the content. There can be no
doubt that Longfield had a very clear grasp of the structure of
Ricardian theory — he recognised the reasons for Ricardo's search
for an invariable measure of value and was able to present the idea
of the inverse wage-profit theorem in a manner which led Torrens
to withdraw his objections to it.[27]

Now if this particular feature of Ricardo's system is to be seen as
the essential one, some of the traces of Ricardian ideas which, as I
have always pointed out, are to be found all through Longfield's
Lectures on Political Economy will assume enhanced significance. Longfield did devote one whole lecture (Lecture VIII) to examining
what profits are, 'and how their amount is to be calculated'. By
assuming all advances of capital to be made in the form of wages
and for the same length of time 'it will follow, that the rate of profit
depends upon the proportion in which the value of any commodity
is divided between the labourer and the capitalist'.[28] This is indeed
a Ricardian way of measuring profits, but when it comes to 'the
investigation of the laws which determine their actual amount'
Longfield's treatment of this question involves a polite but total
refutation of Ricardo's ideas.

Admitting that 'some of the most distinguished writers have
adopted the theory, first, I believe, proposed and explained by the
late Sir Edward West, which considers profits to be almost entirely
regulated by the fertility of the last and worst soil that is brought

127

under cultivation', Longfield declared that 'the theory is an ingenious one, and I should feel much pleasure in assenting to it, and it is with corresponding regret that I have come to the very contrary conclusion, namely, that the decreasing fertility of the soil has scarcely any direct effect upon the rate of profits . . .'.[29]

In the Ricardian system rent is a surplus resulting from the 'indestructible powers of the soil'; of the remainder of the produce the share which goes to the labourer is determined by the cost of his subsistence, and the residue forms the profits of the capitalist. Hence it follows 'that in all countries, and all times, profits depend on the quantity of labour requisite to provide necessaries for the labourers on that land or with that capital which yields no rent'.[30]

In Longfield's system, on the other hand, rent is a surplus indeed, but one which could arise from land scarcity without differences in fertility; profits are determined by the marginal productivity of capital, and the residue is divided among the labourers in accordance with their specific productivity. 'Naturally, therefore, Longfield reaches very different conclusions from Ricardo on the question of how economic progress affects the division of the social product. Superficially his conclusions seem identical with those of the Ricardians, for like them he also predicts a rise in rents, a fall in profits and a rise in wages — but the fall in profits is to be the outcome of increased accumulations of capital, and the rise in wages, of increased productiveness of labour. Longfield enlarges on the favourable social consequences of a low rate of profits, and concludes that in the course of progress the circumstances affecting the state of the labourer will alter "in a manner favourable to his condition". Optimism is substituted for Ricardian pessimism.'[31]

Professor Hollander himself admits that Longfield 'fails to state precisely how his own theory [of profits] was related to the preceding defence of the Ricardian inverse profit-wage relationship' but nevertheless asserts with emphasis that *'it seems clear enough that he envisaged the latter as a valid framework for a satisfactory theory'.*[32] No evidence is adduced to support this assertion, but even if it is accepted at its face value the fact remains that Longfield clearly did not find the Ricardian theory of profits, and the resulting view of the relation between profits and wages in the course of economic growth, satisfactory.

If one accepts, as I am disposed to do, Dr Terry Peach's view of Ricardo's central object of analysis as having been 'specifically to isolate and "illustrate" what he believed to be the only serious basis for a permanent reduction in profitability in the course of capital accumulation — worsening conditions of production on the land',[33] then it is not possible to regard Longfield as anything but non-Ricardian in his analysis of distribution. But what of his analysis of value? We have already seen that Longfield's treatment of the returns to factors of production as determined by the supply of and demand for them prevents him from being regarded as a follower of Ricardo by the members of what I have called the 'dual development' school. On the other hand if one accepts Professor Hollander's view that 'Ricardian economics . . . comprises in its essentials an exchange system fully consistent with the marginalist elaborations'[34] and sets it alongside Professor Moss's view that 'Longfield developed a supply and demand explanation of market price',[35] it would seem that his value analysis added little to what Malthus and Ricardo had already done.

Is it then to be seen as no more than a minor improvement in supply-and-demand analysis, already well understood and accepted by Ricardo, instead of the major departure from his '93% labour theory of value' which it was formerly thought to be?

This is really a combination of two questions; the first is, to what extent was Longfield's analysis of market price an improvement on whatever may have been done by Ricardo in this field. The second, perhaps more fundamental, is, was that analysis merely a supply and demand one, or did it also contain elements of utility theory?

On the first point, there has recently been more than one attempt to reinterpret Ricardo's supply and demand analysis and to show it to have been more complete and consistent, particularly on the question of price-quantity relationships, than has hitherto been recognised. These attempts have served to bring out what one of the reinterpreters has described as the 'formidable interpretative problems engendered by the absence of any systematic treatment of the theory of price in Ricardo's *Principles*'.[36] Consequently the view put forward by commentators such as Rankin and Hollander — that Ricardo held essentially the same ideas about the relations of price and quantity demanded as had been stated by Malthus — has to be inferred mainly from widely separated passages in his pamphlets, letters and speeches.[37]

On the other hand, as Professor Moss has rightly said, 'it was Longfield (and not Ricardo) who made the concept of a demand schedule an integral part of his theory of price'. Nothing in the recent writing on Ricardo's treatment of supply and demand seems to warrant any revision of Moss's judgement that 'Longfield must be credited with having developed one of the earliest and most complete supply-and-demand explanations of market price in British economic thought'.[38]

The second question is the more controversial one. Professor Moss is critical of the idea that Longfield can be regarded as a precursor of the marginal utility approach — an idea which I presented in my 1945 article and which others have also put forward. It seems to me that this is another instance where the answer depends on the criteria adopted — in this case the criteria which make a writer into a utility theorist. If that description is to be confined to those who have given an explicit statement of the principle of diminishing marginal utility it cannot be applied to Longfield, but if the description is extended to include those whose writings make clear their understanding of the principle then it would be my judgement that Longfield would properly come under it. I still would contend that important elements of utility analysis are to be found in Longfield's value theory, which is thus more than a mere supply-and-demand treatment of the problem.

Moss does concede that Longfield 'was quite willing to admit that utility does influence price, but only in the same way as cost of production, that is, *indirectly*. Cost influences market price by way of supply and utility by way of demand because, in Longfield's words, it is to utility that the "demand is to be entirely attributed". But in another place he was quick to warn that the effect utility has on actually determining the market price is "not so easily calculated", and on the basis of this remark we may be confident that Longfield did not intend to connect the "intensity of demand" with a measure of utility'.[39]

This does seem to me to make as little as possible out of what Longfield says about utility and consumer behaviour. Has *any* utility theorist ever tried to show that utility influences price other than 'by way of demand'? Apart from that I do not really see why Longfield's statement that the effect utility has in determining price is not easily calculated ensures confidence that he did not intend to connect intensity of demand with a measure of utility. To my mind the essential point about Longfield's treatment of intensity of demand is that he relates it not merely to market demand but to the demand of the individual consumer.[40]

It seems to me that Professor Bowley's reading of this passage is much more careful and therefore much closer to the truth than that of Professor Moss:

The Irish dissenters

Longfield's exposition of diminishing degrees of intensity of demand provides an explanation of the downward slope of an individual's demand curve, as well as of the market demand curve. It has already been noticed that his degrees of intensity of demand coincide with Dupuit's 'maximum sacrifice' used by him as the measure of utility and the reflection of diminishing marginal utility. Longfield did not take the final step of showing the relation of the concept of intensity of demand to the concept of utility, although he had said that demand 'was to be entirely attributed' to utility. It seems to me then that Longfield introduced the degrees of intensity of demand as a way round the difficulty of discovering the effect of utility on price because although he, like so many others, observed the phenomenon of diminishing utility, he was unable to draw conclusions from it in a way which demonstrated the precise influence of utility on exchange value.[41]

If the matter is seen in this way, Longfield's failure to take the final step explicitly does not seem to me adequate ground for denying that he was a precursor of the marginal utility approach. And the grounds for claiming him as such seem to be strengthened by Moss's own statement that 'Longfield came closer than any of his contemporaries to stating what is now commonly referred to as the "first-order condition" in the theory of consumer choice—that a consumer will vary his purchases of several commodities in such a way that the proportions between their respective marginal utilities and prices will all be equal to one another'.[42] Taking all the evidence into consideration then, it seems to me that even if Longfield did not state the law of diminishing marginal utility explicitly and precisely, it is still reasonable to classify him as a 'utility' or 'subjective value' theorist, and that to treat his theory as no more than a supply and demand one is to give it an unduly narrow interpretation.

V

Finally, we come to consider the view that the Irish dissenters, in line with their English counterparts, were harmony theorists and defenders of the status quo whose opposition to Ricardian distribution theory was partly, if not mainly, founded in a desire to play down those conflicts between classes which it so starkly highlighted. Now one would scarcely expect the early occupants of the Whately Chair to have been radicals, appointed as they were by an Archbishop of the then established Church of Ireland to lecture on political economy in a college whose students were mainly drawn from the ascendancy class and whose revenues derived from extensive landholdings. Nor indeed were they, although Mr Antoin Murphy elsewhere in this volume (pp. 13-24)[43] has drawn together interesting evidence of the proceedings of the Board at the time of the first elections to the Chair which indicates that Longfield was looked at askance by some of the Senior Fellows because of his supposed radical opinions. On the other hand his successor Isaac Butt at the time of his election in 1836 was well known for his high Tory views, views far removed from those he was later to express as leader of the Irish Home Rule party.[44]

Viewed objectively against the background of these facts, the Irish dissenters appear neither as radicals nor as defenders of the status quo but rather as concerned reformers. On some aspects of social and economic policy, notably that of trades unions and combinations, their position was undoubtedly a conservative one.

'Let the labourer be taught to know', declared Longfield, 'and the proof is simple and easy to be understood by all, that the wages of his labour cannot be determined by the wishes of his employer, that they are even as independent of the decrees of the legislature as they are of his own will, and that they are ultimately entirely dependent upon the prudence or improvidence, the industry or idleness, of the labouring classes themselves.'[45]

Professor Hollander has recently suggested that these comments may have been intended as a reply to the radical socialism of Thomas Hodgskin; 'the tone of Longfield's remarks here and his general emphasis upon the rule of law and the limited potential of union activity suggest that he may have been familiar with Hodgskin's writings.'[46] That is possible, but it seems to me much more likely that Longfield's remarks were directed against the Dublin trades unions whose notoriously violent tendencies at that period had earned the condemnation of Daniel O'Connell among others.

It is also Professor Hollander's contention that Longfield provides an instance of one of the dissenters using Ricardian doctrine to counter radical arguments rather than rejecting them because of their radical implications—a neat reversal of the reading of the historical record given by such commentators as Sraffa and Dobb.[47] Again, the significance to be attached to this depends on one's view of the importance of the traces of Ricardian doctrine to be found in Longfield's writings. To my mind it was Longfield's departures from Ricardo's theory of distribution—his reversal of the place of profits and wages in the sharing of the total product and his productivity analysis of their determination—which enabled him to take an optimistic view of the progress of capitalist society and the prospects for labour within it.

However the significant point in this context is not the degree of importance to be attached to the Ricardian elements in Longfield's economic theory. Rather it is the undoubted fact that Longfield gave clear and frequent indication that he was no uncritical defender of the existing order. As Professor Hollander has rightly noted, 'the matter of "undesirable" distribution was placed squarely within the domain of the economist' by Longfield.[48] The position which he took on this question is a specially interesting one. On the one hand in his *Four lectures on Poor Laws*[49] he supported the stern principle, developed by Nassau Senior, of giving aid to the able-bodied only on a basis of 'less eligibility'. On the other he asserted that *every individual is entitled to the means of support from that society which is determined to compel him to obey its laws'.*[50]

The basis for this assertion was that 'society is nothing but a combination of individuals for the common good. Can they with justice (I speak not of compassion now) say, we have divided the land and property of the country among us in a manner that we have found by experience is well calculated to promote our interests, but you have got no share in this distribution, and we do not want your labour, therefore you must starve.' The able-bodied therefore might as of right demand and receive subsistence from the society which demanded their allegiance—but nothing more.

It was always Longfield's view that others less fortunate—'the blind, the insane, the crippled poor' and the aged—in whose case the granting of assistance could involve no risk of encouraging idleness and improvidence should be generously aided by the state. Even in 1834 he was prepared to advocate 'a small pension as a superannuation allowance, to every labourer of sixty years of age'[51] and when in 1872 he came to consider 'The limits of state interference with the distribution of wealth' he 'set out a programme of redistribution of wealth and social investment which anticipates most features of the modern welfare state'.[52]

In this remarkable paper there are interesting anticipations of Keynes in references to 'the average strength of the disposition to accumulate' which Longfield argued to be 'greater than is necessary, and can bear reduction without loss to the public'.[53] Similarly his 1834 discussion of the right to subsistence finds echoes today in current discussions of the 'right to food' which often make reference to Rawls's *Theory of justice.*[54] One criticism which can be made of Longfield, particularly in relation to his 1834 *Four lectures on the Poor*

133

Laws is that he did assume that the able-bodied would normally find no difficulty in obtaining employment through the workings of the labour market—an assumption which was scarcely borne out by the facts in Ireland at that time. It was left to the young Tory barrister who succeeded him, Isaac Butt, to point this out and draw attention to the limitations of an economic theory based on full employment assumptions.

'It appears to me,' he wrote in an unobtrusive footnote, 'that in all the arguments which attempt to prove, as a general proposition, the injury of protective duties, it is assumed that the industry of a country must always be fully employed'.[55] Recognising the restricted validity of this assumption, particularly in pre-famime Ireland, he was prepared to swim against the full tide of orthodox economic opinion and state the case for protection to home industry as a means of increasing employment. The argument by which Butt supported his case is still worth hearing almost a century and a half later:

Enough for us now to state the general principle, that if there be in our own land a state of society in which men are willing to work, and cannot find the opportunity of exchanging their labour for bread, and if the community in which this occurs have resources enough at its command, by the best and most carefully contrived combination of all its skill and power to find bread for all its people, there ought to be an effort made to bring about that result. To this end, if it can be obtained, there is no taxation that might be necessary to accomplish it that ought not cheerfully to be borne—there is no sacrifice from those who own the revenue of the country, too great to demand. In the progress of society, the masses of the people ought surely to have their share. . . These principles and these reasonings may fall strange upon the ear of some present. Be assured, the time is coming when they shall not be so.[56]

Such are some of the writings of the Irish dissenters on the economic situation in their time. They are not, in my judgement, the words of Ricardians but assuredly they are equally not the words of harmony theorists, Pollyannas, or the running dogs of the capitalist class.

VI

The development of economic thought in the nineteenth century was a complex process with many facets—about which we have learned much as a result of the scholarly studies carried out during the last forty years. Inevitably attempts must be made to elucidate the complexity by imposing patterns on it. One such is the 'dual development' thesis, promoted mostly by economists of the Cambridge school since Sraffa, another what may be called the 'general equilibrium' approach of which Hollander is the leading exponent.

According to the first the Irish economists who held the Whately Chair in its early days are to be seen as part of the reaction against Ricardo, forerunners of neoclassical or marginalist economics indeed but tarnished by all the unhappy features which the term 'neoclassical' implies in modern Cambridge thinking. According to the second they become not part of the reaction against Ricardo but of a resilient Ricardian tradition involved in 'the sharing of a common heritage or "central core", which amounts largely to allocation theory and the mechanisms of demand-supply analysis'.[57]

With what may well be regarded as typical Irish stubbornness I have chosen to dissent from both these interpretations; but I hope that I may be judged to have given adequate reasons for my continuing belief that the early Whately professors can be correctly seen as constituting something like a school of their own which had its own original thread to weave into the pattern of nineteenth century economic thought, as regards both theory and policy.

Notes

1. These views are perhaps to be found most clearly and forcefully stated in Edwin Cannan, *A history of theories of production and distribution in English political economy from 1776 to 1848* (London, 1893) and *A review of economic theory* (London, 1929). But cf. also F. H. Knight, 'The Ricardian theory of production and distribution' in *Canadian Journal of Economics and Political Science*, i, (1935), pp 3-25 and 171-96.

2. E.R.A. Seligman, 'On some neglected British economists, I and II' in *Economic Journal*, XIII (1903), pp 335-63 and 511-35.

3. Marian Bowley, *Nassau Senior and classical economics* (London, 1937), p. 67.

4. ibid., p. 109.

5. R.D. Collison Black, 'Trinity College, Dublin, and the theory of value, 1832-1863' in *Economica*, N.S., xii (August 1945), pp 140-8.

6. J.A. Schumpeter, *History of economic analysis* (London, 1954), Part III, ch.4.

7. Mark Blaug, *Economic theory in retrospect* (3rd ed., London, 1978), p. vii.

8. G.A. Caravale and D.A. Tosato, *Ricardo and the theory of value, distribution and growth* (London, 1980), p. 4.

9. Piero Sraffa, Introduction to Vol i of *Works and correspondence of David Ricardo* (10 vols, Cambridge, 1951-73), pp xiviii-ix.

10. M.H. Dobb, *Theories of value and distribution since Adam Smith* (Cambridge, 1973), p. 112.

11. ibid., p. 115.

R. D. Collison Black

12. Samuel Hollander, 'On the substantive identity of the Ricardian and neo-classical conceptions of economic organization: the French connection in British classicism' in *Canadian Journal of Economics*, xv, no. 4 (November 1982), pp 586-612 (pp 590-91).

13. Nevertheless I may be allowed to comment that I do not find either wholly convincing. I would agree with the recently expressed view of Dr T. Peach—'Ricardo's words and intentions have all too often been strained and distorted so that he might be bracketed with "Neoclassical" economists, "Marxist" economists or "Sraffian" economists.'—Terry Peach, *A re-interpretation of David Ricardo's writings on value and distribution* (Unpublished thesis for the degree of D. Phil, University of Oxford, Trinity Term, 1982), p. 241.

14. Dobb, *Theories of value and distribution*, pp 107 et seq.

15. ibid., p. 108.

16. R.L. Meek, *Studies in the labour theory of value* (London, 1956), pp 124-5.

17. Samuel Hollander, *The economics of David Ricardo* (London, 1979), p. 671 (hereafter cited as *E.D.R.*).

18. ibid., p. 277.

19. L.S. Moss, *Mountifort Longfield, Ireland's first professor of political economy* (Ottawa, Illinois, 1976), pp 33 et seq.

20. ibid., p. 97.

21. Samuel Hollander, 'The reception of Richardian economics' in *Oxford Economic Papers*, xxix, no. 2 (July 1977), pp 222-57 (pp 232-3).

22. Mountifort Longfield, *Lectures on political economy, delivered in Trinity and Michaelmas Terms, 1833* (Dublin, 1834), p. 209 (hereafter cited as *L.P.E.*).

23. Hollander, *E.D.R.*, p.7.

24. Hollander, 'Reception of Ricardian economics' in *O.E.P.*, xxix (1977), p. 224.

25. Cf. Samuel Hollander, 'Review of Moss, *Mountifort Longfield*' in *Canadian Journal of Economics*, xi (1978), pp 378-80 (379). In a review of Hollander's *E.D.R.*, Moss has argued that the 'consensus view' of Ricardian theory is that which 'insists that the truly unique or novel element in Ricardo's theorizing was his "agricultural theory of profit" ' (L.S. Moss, 'Professor Hollander and Ricardian economics', *Eastern Economic Journal*, 5, (Dec. 1979) p. 503). Cf. also Hollander, 'Professor Hollander and Ricardian economics: a reply to Professor Moss', *Eastern Economic Journal*, 8 (July 1982), pp 237-41 and Moss, 'Reply to Hollander', *ibid*, pp 243-5.

26. Moss, *Mountifort Longfield*, p. 97.

27. Hollander, 'Reception of Ricardian economics' pp 234-5; Lionel Robbins, *Robert Torrens and the evolution of classical economics* (London, 1958), pp 55-7. Professor Hollander has rightly stressed the influence of Longfield on Torrens, which was not noted in my Introduction to the 1971 reprint of Longfield's economic writings (see below, note 31). On this point see also Moss, 'Professor Hollander and Ricardian economics', *Eastern Economic Journal* 5 (Dec. 1979), p. 505.

28. Longfield, *L.P.E.*, pp 171, 179.

29. ibid., p. 183.

30. Ricardo, *Works and correspondence* (ed. P. Sraffa), i, 126.

31. R.D. Collison Black (ed.) *The economic writings of Mountifort Longfield* (with introduction and bibliography, New York, 1971), p. 16.

32. Hollander, 'Reception of Ricardian economics', p. 235.

33. Peach, *A re-interpretation of David Ricardo's writings. . .*, p. 235.

34. Hollander, 'The French connection in British classicism' in *C.J.E.* xv no. 4 (November 1982), p. 590.

35. Moss, *Mountifort Longfield. . .*, p. 30.

The Irish dissenters

36. S.C. Rankin, 'Supply and demand in Ricardian price theory: a re-interpretation' in *Oxford Economic Papers,* xxxii, no. 2 (July 1980), pp 241-62 (p. 244).

37. Rankin, op. cit., pp 244-54 and Hollander, *E.D.R.,* pp 273-80. On this point cf. also G.J. Stigler's review of Hollander, *E.D.R.* in *Journal of Economic Literature,* xix (March 1981), p. 101.

38. Moss, op. cit., pp. 34, 38.

39. ibid., p. 40.

40. Longfield, *L.P.E.,* p. 115.

41. Marian Bowley, *Studies in the history of economic theory before 1870* (London 1973), pp 152-3.

42. Moss, *Mountifort Longfield,* p. 41.

43. Antoin Murphy, 'Mountifort Longfield's appointment to the chair of political economy in Trinity College, Dublin, 1832', in this volume, pp. 13-24.

44. Cf. Terence De Vere White, *The road of excess* (Dublin 1945).

45. Longfield, *L.P.E.,* p. 19.

46. Samuel Hollander, 'The post-Ricardian dissension: a case study in economics and ideology' in *Oxford Economic Papers,* xxxii, no. 3 (September 1980), pp 370-410 (p. 395).

47. ibid., p. 403.

48. ibid., p. 405.

49. Mountifort Longfield, *Four lectures on Poor Laws,* delivered in Trinity Term, 1834 (Dublin, 1834).

50. ibid., p. 19. Italics in original.

51. ibid., p. 33.

52. Black, *Economic writings of Mountifort Longfield,* p. 25.

53. Mountifort Longfield, 'The limits of state interference with the distribution of wealth, in applying taxation to the assistance of the public' in *Journal of the Statistical and Social Inquiry Society of Ireland,* part xiii (1872), pp 105-114. (Reprinted in Black, *Economic Writings of Mountifort Longfield*).

54. N.J. Faramelli, *World hunger, ethics and the right to eat* (Rome, 1982) pp 7, 8, 13. I am indebted to my son, Mr T.R.W. Black, for drawing my attention to this and other references on the *right to food.*

55. Isaac Butt, *Protection to home industry. Some cases of its advantages considered. The substance of two lectures delivered before the University of Dublin, in Michaelmas term, 1840* (Dublin, 1846), p. 133.

56. ibid., p. 63.

57. Hollander, *E.D.R.,* pp 683-4.

138 - 56

0112
0440
Ireland

Economists and governments: Ireland 1922-52

by Ronan Fanning

'One of the most striking features of Irish politics in recent years', observed Desmond Williams (Professor of Modern History at University College, Dublin) in 1953,

has been the frequency with which politicians employ economic phraseology. Englishmen perhaps would not regard this as something strange; they have been used to it for many years. In Ireland, however, it is probably only since 1948 that ordinary people have appeared to take an interest in economic debate. This is indeed a universal phenomenon; but for a very long time the language of popular appeal in Irish politics was not an economic one. People in pubs and at fairs were more concerned with questions arising out of history and political science. . . The declaration of the republic in 1948-49, however, finished a long chapter in modern Irish politics. . . Since that date, the politicians have adopted 'economics'; they affect an understanding of economic terminology, and are courting the affections and interests of professional economists.[1]

Today, with the benefit of thirty years' hindsight, this perspective has been sharpened rather than blurred. The landmark of 1948 looms larger than ever, even if dwarfed by the still larger landmark represented by the publication of *Economic development* in 1958. Current orthodoxy among historians of twentieth-century Ireland, pointing to the obsessive preoccupation with sovereignty and the British connection so characteristic of the early decades of Irish independence, concurs with F.S.L. Lyons in seeing *Economic development* 'as a watershed in the modern economic history of the country. . . For the classic symptoms of low income per head combined with a consistently adverse balance of payments, Dr Whitaker offered remedies that may at first sight have appeared startling, but were in reality no more than the intelligent application to the local Irish situation of doctrines that had been current among economists elsewhere for many years'.[2] But what of *Irish* economists? Although there is little dispute that what John A. Murphy terms a 'national recovery' hinging upon 'the remarkable economic expansion of the Lemass era'[3] takes place in the late fifties and early sixties, the role of Irish economists in the preceding thirty years has attracted little scholarly scrutiny. Are we to assume, as seems at

138

Economists and governments: Ireland 1922-52

least implicit in the writings of some economic historians, that Irish economists were waiting in the wings, poised to spring on to centre-stage and re-direct the course of Irish society and thus of Irish history, thwarted from doing so only by the successive abnormalities—civil war, depression, economic war, and World War II—which dogged the Irish economy; thwarted, too, some would have us believe by the circumstances which so long delayed Lemass's succeeding de Valera as Taoiseach?[4]

It seems peculiarly appropriate that one of a series of lectures designed to celebrate the 150th anniversary of the chair of political economy in this college should be addressed to such matters if only because the early history of independent Ireland so frequently testifies to the tension between politics and economics—a tension, alas, more stultifying than creative. My purpose, then, is to explore a rather different assumption: that the mentalities of economists in independent Ireland—and of the economists attached to the universities in particular—were not in fact so clearly distinguishable from the mentalities of their educated fellow-citizens with whom they shared common cultural and intellectual attitudes and inhibitions. Such an hypothesis may seem unremarkable, even commonplace and self-evident, yet it is demanded by those constrictions of current orthodoxies which would seek to claim for Irish economists perceptions and perspicacity which they never claimed for themselves.

What follows, then, is no more than an essay in exploration of the relationship between economists and governments in the first decades of independence. I am less concerned to propound conclusions than to chart in outline some of the paths through the Irish intellectual undergrowth which might reward further research and which will at least, I hope, prompt further discussion. My approach, I must stress from the beginning, is simply that of the historian in the general sense of that term—not that of the economic historian, still less that of the economist which I make no pretence of being. Indeed my interest in economists as a breed is akin to that of a zoologist whose attention has been drawn to the habits of an exotic but somewhat neglected species frequenting his native habitat. Or, more appositely perhaps, that of an anthropologist convinced of the significance of a sect of witchdoctors in the tribe which is his present subject of study.

Preliminary examination immediately reveals that the most striking characteristics of the sect are two: exclusivity and longevity. A mere dozen men—it seems almost needless to remark that there were no women—held chairs of economics in the four university colleges of independent Ireland between 1922 and 1958. And that is defining chairs of economics in the broadest sense: whether of Political Economy in Trinity or UCD, or National Economics in UCD, or Economics and Commerce in UCC, or Economics, Commerce and Accountancy in UCG—Maynooth merits mention only in that it had *no* chairs of economics, no witchdoctors within those hallowed portals. If, moreover, one focusses upon the quarter of a century after 1926, the core of our period, the number of a dozen may immediately be halved.

The length of tenure of the principal incumbents is still more remarkable: only one of the holders of the principal chairs of economics in the four colleges when *Economic development* appeared in 1958 had been appointed later than 1932. This was Senator Liam Ó Buachalla who had succeeded to the chair of Economics, Commerce and Accountancy in Galway when his predecessor, Francis McBryan, finally stepped down after a reign of office which had begun in 1919. In UCD, George O'Brien had held the chair of National Economics since 1926 (he subsumed the second chair, of Political Economy, in 1931); in UCC, John Busteed had succeeded Timothy Smiddy even earlier, in 1924; and in Trinity, George Duncan had been appointed in 1932.

In examining these matters in more detail, given the occasion which this series of lectures was designed to celebrate, it would seem singularly ungracious not to turn first to Trinity.

When C.F. Bastable, Professor of Political Economy at Trinity in 1922, was first appointed, the convention was that the chair was part-time with a maximum tenure of five years. That was in 1882 and the break with precedent in 1887, the latest historians of the college tell us,

marks the development of the post from what was in modern terms a post-doctoral fellowship to something more like a real professorship. There was, however, no increase in pay, and Bastable was able to retain it only by virtue of the fact that he held also the chair of Jurisprudence and Political Economy at Queen's College, Galway.[5]

In 1912 Bastable was given a life-tenure which expired only in 1932 after he had held the chair for a full fifty years. His replacement, the same authorities tell us, marked the transformation of economics from a peripheral to a central subject. . . (Duncan) had as acutely critical a brain as any of his generation in the college, and he used it to good effect in his lectures, in which his demolition with surgical skill of the theories of some of his fellow economists delighted at least the first-class men in his audience. . . But he seems to have turned in on himself the same unsparing criticism which he applied to others, for his writings were not commensurate with his ability. . . His only senior colleague . . .was Joseph Johnston, who, having studied both Ancient History and Economics fell badly between the two stools, for he saw junior colleagues appointed to the professorships in both subjects. He then took up farming in his spare time and wrote extensively, if somewhat idiosyncratically on agricultural economics with special reference to Irish problems.[6]

Both Johnston and Duncan were ferociously hostile to the economic policies of the Fianna Fáil governments which held sway throughout the central part of our period (1932-48), again in 1951-54 and again after 1957—a trait which they shared with other university economists of their generation (and with George O'Brien and his acolytes in particular). Indeed one need not go much beyond the sub-title inside the dust-jacket of Johnston's *The nemesis of economic nationalism* (Dublin, 1934)—'Thoughts suggested by a study of the Anglo-Irish experiment in economic vivisection'—to gauge his position with a fair degree of accuracy. 'Unless we wish to go onward to a complete regimentation of all our economic life on Bolshevik lines', he told the Statistical and Social Inquiry Society of Ireland in May 1935, 'we must remove our economic compass from the field of political magnetism, and get back to a régime in which prices reflect, not political ideals, but economic realities'.[7] But political realities, alas, obtruded and continued to obtrude for many years to come.

Duncan was of like mind as we can see from his warm endorsement of George O'Brien's paper on 'Monetary policy and the depression' (expressing extreme scepticism about public expenditure and monetary management as instruments for restoring prosperity) before the same forum a year earlier. O'Brien's paper, declared Duncan, was

wholesomely discouraging to a number of beliefs presently much in vogue. Hitherto the advocates of 'easy money' as a panacea for economic ills had all the publicity. . . The opinions of the more orthodox economists. . . (that hardship to many persons is not only inevitable but. . . necessary) . . .have been complex, revolting to a false sentimentality, and anathema to all kinds of legal, class and nationalistic vested interests.[8]

We shall have cause to return to Duncan again, in regard to his trenchant defence some twenty years later of the Irish universities and their economists. But, for the moment, it is sufficient to remark that the situation here outlined offered no promise of dynamic co-operation between Trinity economists and Irish governments, not-withstanding such episodes as Duncan's participation in the Bank-ing Commission of 1934-38. Indeed, whatever the problems arising from Bastable's half-century tenure of office and whoever the Trinity economists and whatever their accomplishments, to expect that Trinity, for so long the bastion of Protestant ascendancy and trau-matised by the treaty, civil war and now by the advent of de Valera, would prove the forcing-house of economic development in inde-pendent Ireland smacks of an unrealism bordering on the histori-cally anachronistic. The National University of Ireland, on the other hand, given its aspirations and the circumstances of its foun-dation might more reasonably have been expected to crave such a role.

Galway may be speedily disposed of if only because it had no chair of economics *per se* but a professorship of Economics, Commerce and Accountancy. Francis McBryan, appointed in 1919 at the age of thirty-seven to the chair which he was to hold until he was seventy-three, was essentially a commercial teacher who had taught office routine and business methods, commercial arithmetic and book-keeping in Omagh Technical School for seven years, before becoming the Chief Commercial Instructor under the County Mayo Technical Instruction Committee for six years and then Principal of Ballina Technical School. He obtained both his B.A. degrees in Political Economy and National Economics and his Higher Diploma in Education (in 1915 and 1916) as an extern student of University College Dublin while working a full schoolday six days a week as a commercial instructor and travelling by train between the three towns in which his classes were held. Earlier, in 1910-12, he had attended courses of lectures at the L.S.E.

Liam Ó Buachalla, appointed to succeed McBryan in 1953, was no more of a professional economist than his predecessor. He, too, studied in UCD as a student of mature years, beginning the B.Comm. course in 1924 when he was 25 years old. He, too, was a commercial teacher, and in addition, a teacher of Irish and a prominent member of the Gaelic League. This stood him in good stead as he applied for the lectureship in Commerce, Accountancy and Economics (through the medium of Irish) at UCG before he

142

had sat for his degree examination in Commerce. That was in 1927. He duly obtained the position which he held for the next twenty-five years before succeeding to McBryan's chair. Ó Buachalla specialised in the economics of the Gaeltacht and in a contribution to the mid-fifties debate on emigration, argued that 'Ireland is still suffering from the effects of the Act of Union'.[9]

The situation in Cork is deserving of more detailed scrutiny. The first professor, Timothy Smiddy, was something of a polymath: fluent in French and German, having been educated in Paris for four years and in Germany for another year when he took economics courses at the University of Cologne, he had also studied chemistry at Queen's College, Cork and the industrial applications of chemistry as well as economics in Manchester. He became a Fellow of the Chemical Society in 1900 and obtained his M.A. with honours in Mental and Moral Sciences in the Royal University of Ireland in 1908. Between 1901 and his becoming first professor of Economics and Commerce in 1909, he worked in a timber merchants' yard in Cork where he had been managing director since 1905. Smiddy was rare among university economists in that he resigned his chair early, in 1923. He then enjoyed a highly successful career in the public service and he had become intimately involved with the new government in an advisory capacity even before the Irish Free State was established, first on the sub-committee on financial relations established during the treaty negotiations of 1921, and latterly as special adviser to Michael Collins on banking and finance during the provisional government of 1922 when it was his avowed

intention to avoid all political issues, and to express as few opinions of his own as possible, and so to present a report which would consider the question purely from an economic angle. He desired to see that system of banking and currency established in the country which would be best suited to the economic conditions prevailing. . . He thought that the Irish banks were in a sound financial condition, that their banking system was a good one, and that being so, he thought that there should be as few changes as possible in their banking laws, the fewer the better.[10]

Few changes there were and Smiddy was subsequently appointed 'agent for the purpose of studying the methods of public administration in the United States, and looking after the financial interests of the government'. Shortly afterwards, in October 1924, he was accredited as Ireland's first diplomatic representative to the United

States, a position he held until 1929 when he became Irish High Commissioner in London, a post he relinquished in 1930.[11]

Smiddy's subsequent career is still more interesting and the proof of his successfully attaining his aim of avoiding political issues was seen in his becoming de Valera's economic adviser: an economist, that is, in de Valera's own words,

whose views, when financial and other matters came up, I consulted from time to time and with whom I discussed some of these matters as a check upon the views that might be expressed by others—not that his views are going to supersede the views expressed by departmental experts, but just to get an outside independent point of view, which helped from time to time to get a new approach to a particular problem.[12]

I have found few signs of Smiddy's advice in the records released in recent years by the Taoiseach's Department and it may be that we must await the opening of de Valera's own papers before we can learn the extent of his influence, although it would appear to have been most pronounced in the early thirties. He later chaired a commission of inquiry into agriculture in 1938 and was appointed to the first board of the Central Bank in 1943. Already, however, we can say that Cork's first Professor of Economics was unique not only in having the ear of both Collins and de Valera as heads of government but in so successfully making the transition from academic life to the public service. His, certainly, is a career which would repay further study.

Smiddy's successor as Professor of Economics and Commerce in Cork was John Busteed. Busteed was a product of the North Monastery who, in 1913, won the first Honan Scholarship. But an academic career of high promise was interrupted by the Great War when he joined the Irish Guards and, aged twenty-two, he controlled the Guards Division intensive machine gun school at Bisley and 'trained thousands of Life Guards, Horse Guards and London Metropolitan Police', an experience which he claimed to be of 'great practical educational value'. He also was a mature student of twenty-five before, in 1920, he obtained his B.Comm. with First Class honours; and he won the NUI's Travelling Studentship in Economics the following year. His use of the studentship was enterprising if unorthodox: he asked J.J. McElligott (Secretary of the Department of Finance from 1927-53 and assistant secretary from 1923-27 but who was then managing editor of *The Statist* in London) to supervise his researches in practical finance. McElligott, wrote Busteed, arranged his work on *The Statist* of which, incidentally, he became a fulltime employee, so that it brought him 'into direct practical touch with all important financial machinery and current developments'. Busteed claimed that as a member of the Chartered Institute of Journalists he had access to 'information and discussion not available to members of the academic professions'. But Busteed also attended courses at London University on advanced statistics and advanced mathematics and it was this which enabled Smiddy to claim on his behalf that he possessed 'mathematical knowledge and ability of a high order which are of inestimable value to an economist both in the expounding of economic theory and in the analysis and measurement of economic facts' which complemented his ability as a trained statistician—claims which could be advanced for no other economist appointed to a chair in Ireland in the twenties.

What effect this early relationship between McElligott and Busteed had upon their subsequent dealings during the quarter of a century when the former was Secretary of the Department of Finance and the latter Professor of Economics and Commerce at Cork is difficult to say. But that it was McElligott who first served as Busteed's adviser rather than *vice versa* was scarcely irrelevant and such records as I have seen in the Department of Finance do not suggest that McElligott was disposed to call on his erstwhile protegé for advice. Any inclination he might have felt in that direction was doubtless dispelled by Busteed's authorship of the 1934-38 Banking Commission's second minority report and McElligott was particularly incensed when, in 1939, Busteed sent him a memorandum asking whether official policy was prepared to consider the possibility of a break with sterling and committing the heresy of arguing that it was 'no answer to say that in the public interest discussion on such a subject must be confined to anonymous bureaucrats'.[13]

Busteed also had strong views on population problems and, speaking in March 1937, anticipated an accelerated decline of numbers among the white races, especially in Europe; he argued that even in Ireland in the

past two years a remarkable distribution of the literature and knowledge of (contraception) has been quietly proceeding among the middle classes. . .

As far as the Irish Free State is concerned, additional economic privileges given to the family by the state would strengthen the institution of the family, but early action would probably be more potent than delayed action.[14]

145

Busteed made these remarks just when the 1937 constitution, with its heavy emphasis on the role of the family, was being drafted, but whether he was consulted or whether this was a mere coincidence must remain a matter for conjecture.

One further development in Cork requires comment: the establishment of a chair of Economic Theory in 1957 which at first sight might be thought to point to the prospect of innovation. The reality was different. The successful and solitary candidate for what was only a part-time chair was the Rev. W. Paschal Larkin, a Capuchin priest who had acted as Smiddy's substitute in 1921-23 but who had been defeated by Busteed in the contest for the succession. He then served as Busteed's assistant from 1928-36 and subsequently as a part-time lecturer in economics. His appointment was more in the nature of a reward for long service than a new departure and the economic theory entitled in his chair seems to have referred to the theories of Karl Marx and to eighteenth century theories of property. His principal published works were *Marxian socialism*, his travelling studentship thesis published by Cork University Press in 1917, which went through three impressions; and *Property in the eighteenth century* (Cork, 1930).[15]

What, finally, of UCD, the largest constituent college of the National University, seated in the capital, whose economists would appear to have been most favourably placed to sway the ministers and mandarins mere minutes away across Stephen's Green? The first point to be made is that economics at UCD suffered a contraction long before independence when, following Tom Kettle's death on the Somme in 1916, his chair of National Economics went to C.H. Oldham who already held the chair of Commerce. The holder of another economics chair, the celebrated Jesuit, Father Finlay, as a former fellow of the Royal University, was not obliged to retire at a fixed age. Already seventy-three years old when the Irish Free State was established, he was eighty-one when he finally retired in 1930 and his was a career rooted in pre-revolutionary Ireland, in the *New Ireland* of Horace Plunkett. Further contraction occurred when the two economics chairs were combined on his retirement and for the next thirty years held jointly by George O'Brien. James Meenan's fascinating intellectual biography of O'Brien has ensured that we know more about him than about any of his fellow-economists and it would be redundant to retrace all the tracks so elegantly treated within its pages. We should, however, remind ourselves that after a brilliant undergraduate career at UCD culminating in the

146

first-class honours degree in Legal and Political Science, O'Brien
entered the King's Inns and having garnered all their glittering
prizes was called to the Bar in 1913. His legal career was brief and
ended, in 1916, in a nervous breakdown. Only then did he turn to
economics or, rather, to economic history, quickly publishing the
monumental economic histories of Ireland in the seventeenth, eighteenth and nineteenth centuries upon which his subsequent career
rested and for which he was awarded the D.Litt. for published work
in 1919. Economics, as his biographer reminds us, pointing to the
paucity of graduates in the subject, 'had not then become a profession' and O'Brien himself always regarded his academic career 'as
a second best, a comeback after my failure at the Bar, which I
looked at as my first love'.[16]

Given such an intellectual background it is not wholly surprising
that he always remained sceptical of the value of the mathematical
approach to economics which developed during his tenure of office.
Modern economics, he wrote,

has lost some influence by its having become esoteric, a study to be pursued
by the initiated, not comprehended by the general reader. The great
classical economists, like the great historians, were all literary men whose
works were read with pleasure by a wide public. Modern economics and
modern history have taken a wrong turn in the direction of pedantry and
dryness. . . My own leanings have always been in favour of the literary
approach to economic discussion. I have always discussed economic
problems in literary rather than mathematical language. I was a believer
in the liberal, humanistic, tradition expounded so satisfactorily by
Newman.[17]

This unashamed defence of what was essentially descriptive, as
opposed to prescriptive, economics seems as good a point as any on
which to conclude a necessarily hasty survey of the economists of
independent Ireland. We have seen sufficient, however, to appreciate more clearly why it was that Irish economists were scarcely in
a position to command the intellectual deference — and, in some
instances, not even the intellectual respect — of men like Joe
Brennan, J.J. McElligott and John Leydon who effectively ran the
economic and financial machinery of Irish government during the
first thirty years of independence. What distinguished these senior
civil servants not merely from their political masters but also from
Irish academic economists was that their rigorous training in the
British administrative system which they continued to operate had

imbued them with the confidence and conviction that they knew
what needed to be done.

There were other reasons, moreover, why Irish circumstances dic-
tated that economists should fight shy of the perils of prescription
in the immediate aftermath of independence. The inflation and
general economic disruption consequent upon the Great War was
swiftly followed by the indigenous turmoil, first of the war of
independence and then of the civil war. This course of events caused
George O'Brien, writing forty years later, to observe that

the normal life of the country was completely paralysed by the dramatic
happenings in the field of politics. To attempt to give any coherent account
of the economic condition of Ireland during this decade (1912-22) would
baffle the most able economic historian. All the normal standards were in
abeyance, affluence was everywhere sacrificed to defence, and finally the
very unity of the country was disrupted.[18]

Given that what was at issue during the first years of independence
was the very survival of the state rather than the condition of its
economy, there was little temptation for economists to embark upon
the path of rigorous analysis, still less criticism, of the government's
economic policies. The constraints were all the other way and
economists, no less than other elements of society, were infected by
the conservative spirit of the age. Hence the impression, perhaps,
that their role on the various committees and commissions of the
twenties and thirties such as the Fiscal Inquiry Committee and the
Banking Commissions was less to initiate impartial investigations
than to endorse existing government policy.

Another factor which must be taken into account is that the
achievement of Irish independence was not preceded by any real
debate among economists about the economic policies most appropriate in an independent Ireland. There had, of course, been inter-
minable debate about home rule finance, virtually all of which
became superfluous when a much larger measure of freedom than
home rule was achieved and, in the context of the leisurely pace of
academic intercourse at the turn of the century, achieved so quickly.
That there was no coherent body of economic policies designed to
meet such a situation in advance of its achievement accentuated the
advantages enjoyed by the mandarins of Merrion Street.

This is not, of course, to argue that contention, let alone confron-
tation, characterised the relationship between senior civil servants
and academic economists. Brennan, for instance, went directly to

148

the President of UCD and the Provost of Trinity in his efforts to recruit first-class talent directly from the universities—Sarsfield Hogan was the most notable of the recruits who entered the Department of Finance by that unorthodox route which was never again used once formal civil service recruitment procedures had been established. More revealing, perhaps, of how the shaping of dynamic economic policy was crippled by the scarcity of talent in the young state were the endeavours of the Secretary of Industry and Commerce, Gordon Campbell (later Lord Glenavy), to enlist the aid of Professor J.G. Smith of Birmingham University who had earlier served on the Fiscal Inquiry Committee. Following such measures as the amalgamation of Irish railways and the adoption of the Shannon scheme, Campbell was persuaded 'that we have no super-abundance of material resources and that our future progress depends on the genuinely skilled exploitation of such resources as we have'. He wanted to begin inquiries into such matters as the economics of Irish transport; the system of banking and finance; the economics of modern agriculture; the

examination of our national resources, with special reference to the degree in which limitations of quantity, quality, location etc. can be overcome by methods of exploitation discovered and applied in other countries since 1914; (and) devising. . . an economic technology for industry (widely considered, and including agriculture) that would adapt all advanced modern technologies each of which has an essentially national colour, to the special circumstances of Ireland.

His problem, on which he sought Smith's help, was 'how to find the men capable of giving effect to such inquiries. . . within a period of, say twelve months, *and with sufficient authority to compel respect*' (my emphasis). Smith (who had been born in county Cork and educated at Portora and Trinity College, Dublin)[19] was as pessimistic as he was sympathetic and he confessed that he had no idea where Campbell could get the kind of people he wanted:

Such persons have never been politicians, and as there was no career in Ireland during the last twenty years for any but politicians, Ireland has lost the people she needs now. It will be difficult, and almost impossible, to entice them back. I think however, you would get most of what you want by drawing up a kind of questionnaire of each of the broad topics on which you consider an inquiry advisable and then appealing to one or more persons who, in your judgement, are capable of helping.[20]

149

Ronan Fanning

This inquiry approach was, of course, what enabled the government to enlist the aid of such foreign experts as the American Professor of Banking and former Secretary to the Federal Reserve Board, Henry Parker-Willis, during the first Banking Commission and the Swedish economist, Per Jacobsson, during the second. Jacobsson, writing in his diary in 1939, observed that

The Irish economists and almost *all* other Irishmen only know London and England and something of the U.S.A. i.e. all *big* countries. In monetary matters they wanted to make a money market in Dublin—a small London money market. I had great difficulty in convincing them that one could have a central bank without a money market—that neither Sweden nor Switzerland had a money market. I had to try to teach the Irish to take Sweden or Switzerland as their models *and not England.*[21]

Yet, such anglocentricity notwithstanding, Jacobsson enjoyed the special esteem of Brennan and McElligott denied Irish economists—indeed, Seán Lemass derided their attitude to Jacobsson as bordering on the reverential[22]—and his impressions of the Irish economy communicated to the Commission in April 1936 after he had heard a year's evidence are consequently of particular interest.

The weakness of Irish economics were laid bare in Jacobsson's criticism of the fact that he had

found here in the Saorstat no co-ordinated annual review of the financial position of the country. . . In a country where so much is heard about planning, one ought at least obtain from the authorities the full facts regarding their own financial position with a full estimate of the financial results of the various public activities. We know that there is in fact very little real public information about these matters, that there is no public feeling with regard to them, that there is no real co-ordination of policy. . . It should be somebody's position to review the whole situation. . . There must be some permanent organisation whose business it should be to continue the studies which have begun and see that government departments are acquainted with the main facts as to the balance of payments, national income, etc.[23]

A modest enough proposal, it would seem, after fourteen years of independence, yet another thirteen years were to elapse before the government decision of 1949 to establish a Central Statistics Office; and even then its implementation was postponed by a classic bureaucratic brawl about whether or not the Office should be attached to the Taoiseach's Department.[24]

150

Economists and governments: Ireland 1922-52

Statistics and how economists should use them provoked controversy between university economists and some of the more brilliant statisticians working in the public service—men such as Dr Roy Geary who became the first head of the Central Statistics Office and who already enjoyed an international reputation, and Dr M.D. McCarthy who succeeded him in that office and who subsequently became President of University College, Cork. The debate took place largely within the confines of the Statistical and Social Inquiry Society of Ireland which was then the only forum where civil servants felt free to participate on equal terms with university economists and which played a key role in ventilating discussion of Keynesian economics in an Irish context from the early forties.[25]

In October 1942, for example, George O'Brien's presidential address on 'economic relativity' triggered just such a debate. O'Brien complained that 'economists, who may be regarded as the medical advisers of society and reprobated because of the ill-health of their patients, even when that ill-health is a result of a weak constitution, of dissipation, of debauchery and indulgence in every noxious vice', and he questioned the value of statistics as a prescription for recovery. Geary declared his 'profound' disagreement, pointedly suggesting that O'Brien's 'authorities on statistics generally seem unaware of the scope and possibilities of modern statistical method' and arguing in opposition to O'Brien's Pontius Pilate-like fatalism, that 'the most useful present function of the economist would have been to define the types of statistics to be collected and to agitate loud and long for more, better and fresher statistics'. But George Duncan immediately rushed to O'Brien's defence, claiming that 'statistical analysis is an indispensable handmaid of a full economic theory—but still a handmaid. No amount of collection and contemplation and manipulation of statistical data will of themselves ever advance by one iota our knowledge of economic behaviour'.[26]

Geary succeeded O'Brien as president of the society in 1946-50, and his presidency witnessed a succession of seminal papers including, for example, T.K. Whitaker's 'Ireland's external assets' in 1949. But the record of the society's debates in these years reveals a remarkable absence of contributions from university economists and suggests that they were retreating to the loftier pinnacles of their ivory towers. In March 1949, for instance, when Gerhard Tintner of the Department of Applied Economics at Cambridge read a paper on the 'scope and method of econometrics'—the first such paper ever read before the society—not a single university economist contributed to the discussion which was dominated by Geary and W.A. Honohan from the Department of Finance.[27]

The debate was resumed at the society's symposium on 'national income and social accounts' in January 1952 when Dr. M. D. McCarthy of the Statistics Office launched what Professor Duncan at least interpreted as a frontal attack on the universities and their economists when he referred to the usefulness of the Society as a forum for criticism of the conventions employed by those responsible for computing national income statistics:

If these 'rules' have shortcomings from the point of view of the economists, it is then up to them to say so and their criticisms must be constructive and not merely destructive. . . Though the absence hitherto of any criticism whatsoever of this aspect of the work might be taken as a compliment to the work of the compilers, it is far more likely to be due to lack of interest among those who have the duty and should have the ability to provide such criticism. If what is given in the tables is not conceptually correct from the economists' point of view, it is up to them to say so. They need not add that it is impossible to produce the relevant figures for, to the statistician, the 'impossible' is only a little more difficult to attain than the possible.

Duncan's defence of what he called 'the universities and economists of this country' in fact revealed how limited their aspirations were. Having pointed out the difference in terms of resources between the Central Statistics Office 'and the position of an ordinary university Department of Economics, particularly in the Irish Republic' he declared that

the only Irish university which has even a hope of organising research on the factual side of the economy is the Queen's University of Belfast. In Dublin University we have not even one full-time economist. Of our three part-time economists, each has been or is seriously burdened with public work on top of a heavy load of teaching and administration. We have a full-time statistician but he is over-loaded with teaching. Furthermore, local econometrics cannot be the sole interest of practising economists. My interests, for example, are quite different—and that is as it should be. I quite agree that the universities in the Republic should do more about local econometrics—but that is a question not of lack of interest but of lack of staff and money.

Geary joined the fray, leaving

Professor Duncan to his conscience in his remarkable comparison of what he apparently regards as the liberal endowment of the Central Statistics Office with that of Trinity College, Dublin. For all the relevance the

152

comparison has, he might have added that the Taj Mahal cost so many lakhs of rupees. Here, anyway, is the spectacle of a Professor of Economics calling the attention of taxpayers to the relatively generous endowment of the country's Central Statistics Office... We in the Office will be well content to let the public judge if they are getting value for their money having regard to the particular fact that its national audit costs it 0.03 per cent of the national income...

Professor Duncan says that social accounts (which include all economic statistics and which are a liberal education in the working of the economy) are but a 'tiny part' of economics. I can only say: 'More's the pity!' I cannot help wondering if Professor Duncan has greater faith in the methods of pure economics for the solution of the practical economic problems which beset us, than he has in statistics. When economists have to deal with these problems we do not hear much about marginal utility, imperfect competition, utility curves and the rest: they look for the statistics like the rest of us, and what they write is indistinguishable from what the statistician writes, if he can only write as well... We will be glad to have the help of economists in improving statistical method and augmenting the corpus of statistics. Irish students of economics are welcome in the Central Statistics Office: we will indeed stretch our resources to the limit to help them. We offer them a place on the statistical band wagon (or juggernaut chariot, if you will), but if they continue to sulk in their tents we must travel alone.[28]

It says something for the significance of this occasion that copies of the written contributions have found their way into the surviving papers of Patrick McGilligan, Minister for Finance in the first inter-party government which not only established the Central Statistics Office but which initiated the most dramatic shift in direction of government economic policy (and of how that policy was formulated) since independence.[29] I have written in my study of the Department of Finance of the role played by T.K. Whitaker and Patrick Lynch, in particular, and papers released since then have tended to confirm rather than to contradict that impression.[30] Indeed it is arguable that Lynch's translation from the Department of Finance to the Department of the Taoiseach where he worked as economic adviser to Costello was the most important single step in the process whereby Keynesian economic policies came to be implemented by Irish governments.

Lynch was much more than an economic adviser in the *ad hoc* sense in which, as we have seen, Smiddy had acted as an adviser to de Valera. Knowing the system and working within the system, his easy access to Costello meant that he was ideally placed to execute his self-proclaimed belief that 'the economist... must urge the acceptance of new ideas sooner rather than later'. Space does not allow for more than one example, namely a brief four and a half page 'Note on Public Finance' which he prepared in January 1949 and in which he argued that

the basic defect in this country's economy is chronic under-investment. Statistical proof of this condition exists but so far it has received no official recognition. We have resources idle in land, labour and capital. . . Private enterprise unaided by public investment cannot, manifestly, secure any large scale expansion of the Irish economy.

Our present methods of public finance will perpetuate this condition of chronic under-investment. Our public finance technique is antiquated. Our budgetary technique is based on nineteenth century myths and fictions. . . The balanced budget covering both current and capital items is. . . a dangerous fetish in. . . circumstances which. . . exist in Ireland today. . .

A sound policy for full employment of men, land and capital requires two separate budgets annually. . . social profit in the planning of public expenditures must be the criterion for the annual capital budget. The two-budget system is not, in any sense, a device to disguise a deficit with respectability. . . Large-scale public investment has to be correlated with private investment. This presupposes careful planning and government direction. It would seem to require the establishment of a National Investment Board.[31]

Even this truncated summary of parts of Lynch's paper allows us to discern in embryo much of what lay ahead: the first capital budget of 1950, the Capital Investment Advisory Committee, *Economic development* and the Programmes for Economic Expansion. But I have already written at some length of the origins of *Economic development*[32] and have nothing to add to what I said there although it might be helpful to repeat that the first appointment of an economist *qua* economist in the Department of Finance (Dr Brendan Menton) also took place in 1950.[33]

In sum then, it is impossible to absolve university economists from Geary's charge of sulking in their tents clutching to the tenets of pre-Keynesian creeds. Geary returned to the subject some twenty years later—and after a plan to create a college professorship of statistics for him in UCD had collapsed.

The entities in economics are very much social entities, employment, prices, profits, foreign trade and all the rest, yet these are still treated in a somewhat academic way in the university. . . A compromise is effectible between the intellectual discipline of economics as conceived in the university and the needs of the market-place. . . The larger task here is to bring home the pressing need to heads of economic departments, to make an impact on their traditionalist ideas, in many cases to change their philosophy of life. . . There is a gap to be bridged between university discipline and the needs of the community.[34]

And that gap in part explains the central conclusion of this paper: that the winds of change in Irish economics blew vigorously in the corridors of the public service long before the faintest zephyr disturbed the tranquility of the groves of academe. The breeze was first felt, perhaps, in UCD at least, in 1951 when three statutory lectureships were added to the strength of George O'Brien's grossly understaffed economics department. The posts were filled by James Meenan, Patrick Lynch and John O'Donovan. O'Donovan, like Lynch, came from the public service (the Department of Finance) and, like Lynch, his impact upon economics in UCD was subsequent to, if not consequent upon, his experience in government.[35]

But it would be churlish to conclude without acknowledging the difficulties under which academic economists laboured in the early decades of independence. Under-staffed and under-financed, they had latterly to contend with rising student numbers. Nor was the intellectual ambience of independent Ireland—perhaps anti-intellectual ambience is more apposite—appropriate to the practice of economics; not, at least, if social and economic progress is recognised as a legitimate object of economic thought. What I have elsewhere described as the mutually reinforcing political and episcopal visions of an Irish-speaking and Catholic Arcadia rooted in a Golden Age in the past under-pinned the predominant strain of anti-materialism in the political culture of independent Ireland.[36] And anti-materialism and economic development made strange bedfellows.

Yet, whatever the disadvantages with which they had to contend, it seems indisputable that by the early fifties, if not before, the professional economists at least shared many of the weaknesses of two other élites: the most senior civil servants and front-bench politicians. All were of the generation which came to power and influence in Ireland between 1922 and 1932. That each élite by then constituted a gerontocracy hidebound by their past and with little to offer for the future may be a matter for regret; it is hardly a matter for surprise.

Notes

1. T.D. Williams, 'The politics of Irish economics' in *The Statist*, 24 Oct. 1953, pp 23-4.
2. F.S.L. Lyons, *Ireland since the famine* (London, 2nd edt, 1973), p. 628.
3. John A. Murphy, *Ireland in the twentieth century* (Dublin, 1975), pp 142-4.

155

Ronan Fanning

4. See especially Joseph Lee, 'Society and culture' in *Unequal achievement—the Irish experience 1957-82* (Dublin, 1982), pp 1-18.

5. R.B. McDowell and D.A. Webb, *Trinity College Dublin 1592-1952: an academic history* (Cambridge, 1982), p. 314.

6. Ibid., p. 460.

7. *Journal of the Statistical and Social Inquiry Society of Ireland* (hereafter JSSISI), 15(1934-35), p. 80.

8. Ibid., 15(1933-34), pp 1-14.

9. Ibid., 19(1955-56), pp 117-20.

10. Cf. Ronan Fanning 'The impact of independence' in F.S.L. Lyons (ed.) *Bicentenary essays—Bank of Ireland 1783-1983* (Dublin, 1983), p. 68.

11. S.P.O. S 1983A & S 2331.

12. Maurice Moynihan (ed.) *Speeches and statements by Eamon de Valera 1917-73* (Dublin, 1980), pp 562-3; 21 Nov. 1951.

13. Ronan Fanning, *The Irish Department of Finance 1922-58* (Dublin, 1978), pp 365, 374-5.

14. JSSISI, 15(1936-37), p. 63.

15. I am grateful to Ms Noirin Moynihan of the Registrar's Office in the National University of Ireland for providing me with the *curricula vitae* of the early incumbents of economics chairs in the N.U.I.

16. James Meenan, *George O'Brien—a biographical memoir* (Dublin, 1980), pp 146, 158.

17. Ibid., pp 164-5.

18. George O'Brien, 'The economic progress of Ireland 1912-62' in *Studies* (Spring 1962), p. 9.

19. I am grateful to Ms Clara Cullen for this reference.

20. University College Dublin Archives Department (hereafter UCDA), P35b/5.

21. Quoted in E.E. Jucker-Fleetwood, 'Many thanks, Mr Chairman—the Irish Banking Commission 1934-38 as seen by Per Jacobsson' in *Central Bank of Ireland Quarterly Bulletin* (Winter 1972), pp 80-1.

22. I owe this information to Mr Brian Farrell.

23. UCDA P35a/16.

24. See SPO CAB 2/10/196-7, 247; also S 14336B/1.

25. Cf. Fanning, *Department of Finance*, pp 384-5.

26. JSSISI, 17 (1942-43), pp 1-40.

27. Ibid., 18 (1948-49), pp 161-77.

28. Ibid., pp 494-515.

29. Cf. Fanning, op. cit., chapter 10.

30. See the government and cabinet minutes and related files for 1948-51 released by the Taoiseach's Department in 1983 and now available in the State Paper Office.

31. UCDA P35a/FC4.

32. Fanning, op. cit., chapter 11.

33. Ibid., pp 555-6.

34. R.C. Geary, 'The university as an organ in society' in *Exchange* (1964), 4, 1, pp 21-5; I am grateful to Dr Seán Barrett for drawing my attention to this article.

35. Meenan, *George O'Brien*, p. 203.

36. Cf. Ronan Fanning, *'The four-leaved shamrock': electoral politics and the national imagination in independent Ireland* (Dublin, 1983), p. 16.

0322
Edgeworth, Francis Y. 157-74

Francis Ysidro Edgeworth

by Sir John Hicks

I am a little embarrassed by the task that has been laid on me, to speak of F.Y. Edgeworth in this series of lectures on Irish economists. I am not at all sure that he can be reckoned to have been an Irish economist. It is true that he was born in Ireland, and brought up in Ireland; but he rarely speaks of Ireland in his works. When one thinks that he is going to do so, he usually turns off to some other subject. There is however a good deal to be said about his Irish background. I shall allow myself to talk about that at some length, before I come to his economics.

But perhaps I ought to make clear, before I come even to that, that I feel myself to have a rather special relation to him. I had no personal contact with him. I think I once saw a figure on the other side of a street, and was told that it was Professor Edgeworth; that is all. I did not start to work at all seriously on economics until after he was dead. But then quite soon afterwards, really quite soon after he was dead, I found myself drawn to him. Much of my own early work on economic theory is a continuation of his. So I got to think of him, almost as if he had been my teacher. It was in his footsteps that I was trying to walk.

Years later I had the honour (I hope you will understand from what I have just said how great an honour I felt it to be) of succeeding him, at two removes, as Drummond Professor of Political Economy in Oxford. That carried with it, for me as it had done for him, a Fellowship at All Souls College. He was Fellow of the College for thirty-five years, from 1891 to his death in 1926; I have followed him, so far, for thirty-one years, since 1952. We have a splendid photograph of him, which hangs in our common room, and which I have had copied; but for the rest I have not found it easy to collect recollections of him.[1] It is quite a long time ago.

---

[1] I have to make acknowledgements, for help received in the biographical parts of this paper (1) from my colleague, Mr J.S.G. Simmons, formerly librarian of the Codrington Library, All Souls (2) from Mrs Christina Colvin, herself a descendant of Michael Pakenham Edgeworth, Frank Edgeworth's full brother, who is now living in Oxford and has done much work on the Edgeworth family papers, and (3) from Raymond Carr, Warden of St Anthony's College, who is an expert on the nineteenth-century history of Spain.

Sir John Hicks

There are one or two things which our college archivist has been able to collect for me, and one or two which I have got from other sources in Oxford; I shall make use of them later. But in the main I have had to rely on Keynes's well-known memoir, supplemented by the *Black Book of Edgeworthstown*, the history of the Edgeworth family. Keynes knew him well, since for years they were joint editors of the *Economic Journal*. I don't think that Keynes had much sympathy with Edgeworth's approach to economics; he had little understanding of those parts of Edgeworth's work which now seem to be of particular importance. But for Edgeworth as a person he is the source on whom we have most to rely.

Now for the family history, which indeed is an Irish story. One need not go further back than his grandfather, Richard Lovell Edgeworth, a remarkable figure, quite an ornament of the age of Burke and of Grattan, one of the more distinguished periods of Irish history. He had inherited the family estate at Edgeworthstown, County Longford, and lived there a good part of his time. But he made visits to England, finding his way to Lichfield, where he became a member of that notable group of literary people, scientists and inventors, which was a focus of the technological revolution then taking place. He was himself a bit of an inventor; his inventions, though unsuccessful, were quite forward-looking. He organised a semaphore, ancestor of the telegraph; and he tried to make a caterpillar-wheeled vehicle which could climb over walls. But he is best known for his progressive views on education, where he began as a follower of Rousseau, but turned, by experience, into something not less original, but more sensible.

He had a lot of experience, for he married four times, successively, and by each of his wives he had a family, eighteen children in all. So he had quite a school of his own to educate. But they can never have been in his school together; there were too many years between them. Maria Edgeworth, the novelist, came from the first of these families; there is no doubt, you will know, that she belongs to Ireland. (She was said, at the time, to have done for Ireland what Walter Scott was to do for Scotland.) She was thirty years older than her half-brother Frank (Francis Ysidro's father) who came from the fourth family.

But before coming to him, I would like to say a word about another descendant. One of Maria's (full) sisters was the mother of Thomas Lovell Beddoes, that strange but rather appealing figure, who wrote poems that one likes to think as having the same relation to Shelley's as Webster's to Shakespeare's. He died, by his own

Francis Ysidro Edgeworth in 1892 (by courtesy of the Warden and Fellows of All Souls College, Oxford).

hand, when Francis Ysidro was two years old; there is something appropriate in the fact that they were both of them grandsons of Richard Lovell.

I turn to the other side of Francis Ysidro's ancestry. His mother was Spanish (that is where the Y for Ysidro comes from); but I suppose we may now say that that need not make him any less Irish. The story of how his parents met is romantic.

The year (this is important) is 1831. Frank Edgeworth was then 22 years of age. As a very much younger son of so large a family, he did not have much money. But he had managed to visit Italy. On returning to London, with the intention of setting out on further travels, he was shown, by mistake, into a room that was full of ladies. 'They proved to be the wife and daughters of General Eroles, a Spanish exile.' (That is what the *Black Book* says.) Being an Irishman, he came back next day, with a bouquet; and three months later he had married Rosa Eroles, then aged sixteen.

Now just who was this 'General Eroles' and why was he exiled? I was intrigued by this story, and wanted to discover more about it. With the aid of my friends in Oxford, I have had some success; though there are puzzles, important puzzles, which remain. I would like to report on our investigations.

There have been others who have wanted to find out about the Eroles family, in the first place, very naturally, the Edgeworths themselves. There is extant a letter, dated December 1831, addressed to Charles Edgeworth, Frank's half-brother, of the third family. It is written by Lord Holland, the nephew of Charles James Fox, at whose table the Whig leaders, then in office (the Reform Bill ministry) were so often entertained. Charles had appealed to him for information about these people with whom his brother had got entangled. What he says is: 'I took great interest in the fortunes of Madame Eroles and her daughters at the time her husband somewhat imprudently engaged in the expedition of his countrymen against Ferdinand's government a year and a half ago. . . I am much mistaken if either her father (or uncle)-in-law was not the Baron d'Eroles who commanded a very considerable corps in Catalonia during the revolutionary war and was constantly in communication with our naval commanders.' That is what he says; but I think it can now be shown that he was, just a bit, mistaken.

The Baron, who 'collaborated with the British', is a well-known historical figure. He was in fact what we should now call a resistance leader; he led the popular resistance against Napoleon's invasion, in Catalonia, in the foothills of the Pyrenees. His first name was

160

Francis Ysidro Edgeworth

Jaoquin. Now it has been ascertained by my friend the archivist (from the 1886 edition of Burke's Landed Gentry, which contains a note on the Edgeworth family) that the name of Rosa Edgeworth's father was Antonio. So we can separate them out; we have their names.

Lord Holland clearly thought that Jaoquin was Antonio's father (or uncle); but it is known that Jaoquin was born in 1781, so that is not possible. We may take it from him that they were related; it would seem most likely that they were brothers. I shall assume they were brothers.

But now for the puzzle. Jaoquin died in 1825; but before he died he had played a part in the Spanish Civil War of 1823, between so-called 'liberals' and supporters of King Ferdinand's government—which was commonly regarded, in England, as the most disreputable of the 'absolutist' governments which had been established, in many continental countries, during the post-Napoleonic Restoration. In that Civil War, Jaoquin, quite definitely, had been on the absolutist side. But Antonio, as we know from Lord Holland, had taken part in a quite abortive expedition, apparently in 1830, *against* Ferdinand's government. Though that expedition was thought, by Lord Holland, to have been 'imprudent', he evidently sympathised with it; he was prepared to help people who had taken part. So while Joaquin had been pro-Ferdinand, Antonio, it appears, was on the other side.

There is no reason why brothers should not have political differences; but this, surely, is rather extreme. I can only guess at an explanation; but there does not seem to be one possible clue. There was an insurrection in Catalonia in 1827, of people who had been pro-Ferdinand in 1823, but who considered that they had not been properly treated by the party they had supported, when it came out on top. Suppose that Antonio had been involved in that insurrection, went into exile after its failure, and so was available to take part in the expedition of 1830 which started from England. That it meant joining up with people against whom Joaquin had been fighting in 1823 would then be intelligible.

Perhaps, after all, there is a basic consistency. Say that the Eroles were neither leftist nor rightist, even in the terms of that time. What they stood for was Catalan independence, of some sort, from Madrid. That would fit, each time. They were always anti-Madrid, whoever was in power at Madrid. There were some Catalans, already, who took that line. Their stronghold was in the Pyreneean foothills; that was the region where Joaquin, in both of his wars,

161

had his strength. These people kept up their struggle against Madrid, for many years; later on it was to take the form of support from the Carlist pretender. It was a conservative provincialism which did not have much in common with the Catalan nationalism, based on Barcelona, which has been a force in the present century.

I beg pardon for this digression, which has got quite out of scale. Let us go back to Frank and Rosa. They spent the first years of their married life in Florence, then in London; but afterwards they came back to Edgeworthstown, where Francis Ysidro was born in 1845. His father died the next year, but his mother not until 1864. So he must have been brought up by his mother, his education (so Keynes tells us) being given by tutors, from whom he got the Greek and Latin which in his writings he so often displays. And there are other things in his works which reflect that background, as we shall see.

He had one year, here at Trinity College Dublin, in 1862. He afterwards went to Balliol College, Oxford, graduating with a first in 'Greats' in 1869. So his formal education, throughout, was classical; but the substance of his work is mathematical, not classical. Where did he get his mathematics?

I wonder if he was quite self-taught. Anyone who was so mathematically minded as he was, who enjoyed mathematics as he did, must surely have had something of mathematics in his education. He was much more of a natural mathematician than his great contemporary Marshall, who had been a Senior Wrangler at Cambridge, had taught mathematics, and had even thought of becoming a mathematical physicist. Marshall is always putting mathematics away from him; he did not have the affection for it that Edgeworth had. He would never have wanted to campaign for the applicability of mathematics to economics.

I don't see that Edgeworth could have had opportunity, or encouragement, to study mathematics in Oxford; but I wonder about that year at Dublin. There were, in those days, great mathematicians in Dublin. There was Sir William Rowan Hamilton, whose reputation, great at that time, has become even greater since. There must be few modern students of advanced mathematics, or of mathematical physics, who do not know his name. In 1862 his health was failing; but we know that he had some relations with the Edgeworth family, so one would guess that when the boy went to Trinity, he would have been given an introduction to Hamilton. Hamilton was not only a mathematician; he was also a remarkable linguist. If Edgeworth went and talked with him, something could

Francis Ysidro Edgeworth

have happened. There was also George Salmon. I have read Salmon's books; I was lucky to pick up a set of them on one of my early visits to Dublin. I can imagine Edgeworth getting from Salmon something like what I myself, at much the same age, got from G.H. Hardy. Salmon was a beautiful expositor; a pupil of his could well have been in love with curves.

But enough of such conjectures. Though one can only guess how Edgeworth's mathematics started, how his economics started is perfectly clear. It was from Jevons. After Edgeworth had graduated, he went to live in London, nominally reading for the bar, but in fact going on with the philosophy, which he had been doing for 'Greats', and gradually turning from that to statistics and economics. When Edgeworth arrived in London, Jevons was still at Manchester; but his *Theory of political economy* (1871) was a link between the Utilitarianism, to which Edgeworth was already committed, and economics—mathematical economics. From 1876 to 1881 Jevons was professor at University College, London. He then lived in Hampstead, where Edgeworth also was living; we know that they used to go for walks on the Heath together. The preface to Jevons's second edition of his *Theory* (1879), in which he gives references to predecessors and contemporaries, obviously served as a reading-list for Edgeworth's first publication on economics—*Mathematical psychics* (1881).

I shall have much more to say on that book (*MP* I shall call it); but let me first proceed to fill in the main lines of biography. Jevons died, in a bathing accident, in 1882; how far he had had time to read *MP* before he died may be doubted. One must however suppose that it was by Jevons's influence that Edgeworth got his first teaching job in economics, at what was then the only other college of London University, King's. He taught there during the eighties, and during the eighties his reputation mounted, so that we find him, already in 1889, President of Section F (the economics section) of the British Association. Then came the great year of 1891, which set course for the rest of his life. He then went to Oxford as Drummond Professor, and at much the same time became editor of the *Economic Journal*—the first editor of that Journal, only just established. He remained as sole editor until 1911, when he handed over to Keynes. There were some later years when they were joint editors. His work for the *Journal* was a great part of his life.

So from 1891 he was living in Oxford, in rooms in All Souls. (He never married.) He kept his lodgings in Hampstead, and used to come to Ireland in the summer, staying (so Keynes informs us) at the St George Club, Kingstown. In his later years the Edgeworths-

Sir John Hicks

town house came into his possession, as the last surviving direct male descendant of Richard Lovell, but he never lived there. Soon after he died it passed away from the family.

I now turn to his work, and chiefly to that early work *MP*, which seems to me to be the centre of his contribution to economic theory. As will have been seen, he went on writing for forty years after that; but his later writings on economics, though they have their own value, and always their charm, are not often constructive like *MP*. They are mostly of the nature of reviews; even the longest are mainly review-articles. There was no other economist, of his period, who read so much of what was appearing, in many countries and in many languages. One must remember that in those days few writings on economics were translated. The modern economist can draw on the world, even if he knows no language but English; but it was not so then. (It was not so even in my own young days, when one had to read German at least to keep up to date; but it is now many years since I have reviewed a book in German.) So Edgeworth's reviews, and review-articles, which are brought together in the three volumes of his *Papers*, are invaluable to the student of the economics of that period. One can read him on Marshall, on Walras, on Pareto, on Böhm-Bawerk, on Fisher, on Cassel; and since it is the same mind that is reflecting on each of them, he ties them together.

But now for *MP*. The curious title, *Mathematical psychics*, was of course intended as a contrast to mathematical physics, already enjoying the vast reputation which it has retained. He is out to show that similar methods can be applied to human studies also. That nowadays needs no defence; so I need not pay attention to the challenge with which he begins. The substance of what he has to say is in what follows: a chapter on positive economics (economical calculus he calls it) and one on what he calls utilitarian calculus (what we should now call welfare economics). To have made a clear distinction between these two branches was the first, and not the least, of Edgeworth's contributions to economic theory. There is no doubt that he made it; I don't think there is anyone who can be claimed to have made it before.

What he has to say on the positive side is confined, almost entirely (in *MP*) to the theory of exchange—that is to say, if one uses the distinction that comes from Adam Smith, the determination of market prices. He does not go on to production theory, even to the determination of the prices of products; one supposes that he was leaving that to Marshall, with whose early work in that field he was

164

Francis Ysidro Edgeworth

already acquainted when he wrote *MP*. To a Jevonian the market price question came first. One can take it that it was already accepted that in a free market price was determined by demand and supply; that the equilibrium price was that which would bring demand, at that price, and supply at that price, into equality. But just how, and why, would such an equilibrium price be established?

Jevons had seen that this was a question, but had failed to answer it. Walras also had seen it, but had found himself obliged to introduce a fictitious character (modern writers about Walras call him an 'auctioneer', though he is not what I would call an auctioneer) in order to solve it. He is definitely not one of the parties trading. Edgeworth, very properly, would not accept this obviously 'ad hoc' solution. His market has no auctioneer; but if there is enough competition, it does come to equilibrium. He was thus obliged to define, very carefully, what he meant by 'enough competition'.

He begins with a case in which there is no competition, on either side, and then builds up. Then there are just two parties trading, in two commodities; so one of the parties is seller of A and buyer of B, the other is seller of B and buyer of A. Any particular bargain is the exchange of some quantity of A for some quantity of B; so these quantities can be represented by the simple Cartesian co-ordinates of a point on a diagram. If one assumes (as Edgeworth assumed, and it is clearly the general case into which others can be fitted), that each party has some use for each of the commodities traded) we can take it that the seller of A will not give up any A unless he is offered some B in exchange for it; and it is likely that there are other 'bad' bargains which will be similarly refused. For he would then give up what is worth more to him than what he is offered in exchange for it. So one can mark out a region on the diagram, representing those bargains which are impossibly bad from the point of view of the seller of A; and a corresponding region on the side of the seller of B. Any bargain which falls into either of these regions will be rejected, either by one party or by the other. He will prefer to stay where he was, without trading.

The boundaries of these regions are what Edgeworth called *indifference curves;* it was in this context that he invented that name which has become so famous. If either accepted a bargain which was representable by a point that was *on* his indifference curve, he would be not better off (and no worse off) than if he stayed where he was without trading—in the position that is represented by the origin of the diagram. So the indifference curves pass through the

165

origin; and it makes sense to suppose them to curve round, as shown in Figure 1.

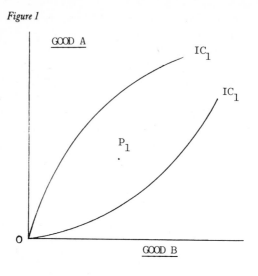

Figure 1

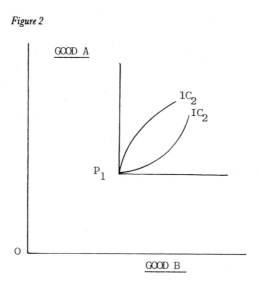

Figure 2

Francis Ysidro Edgeworth

The region between the two boundaries is the region of *practicable bargains*. There is no reason, for anything that has been said so far, why it should not be a wide region. Any point within that region represents a bargain which would give some advantage to each party (over no trading); so if it were to be proposed, and nothing better were on offer, it might be accepted.

But why should nothing better be on offer? Suppose that some bargain, within the practicable region (as shown) were accepted, why should not that be taken as a base for further trading? The possibilities of that can be shown on the diagram. We can take the point P_1, which has been reached in the first bargain, as a new origin, and through that we can draw another pair of indifference curves (Figure 2). Since P_1 was preferred to O, by both parties, any point that is preferred to P_1, by both parties, must also be preferred by both to O; so the practicable region, marked out by the new indifference curves must lie within the old. Suppose that some supplementary bargain, leading to a point within the new practicable region, is accepted. The construction can then be repeated, with a second supplementary bargain, and so on. Each time the practicable region that remains gets smaller; so in the end it must disappear. There is then no opportunity for supplementary trading.

That is as far as one can get, without competition. It is no more than the first step in Edgeworth's theory. It is however already shown, by this process of supplementation, that many of those bargains which appeared at the first round to be practicable, are not practicable as *final* bargains. All those that remain can be shown to lie on a curve, which Edgeworth called the *contract curve*. Once the contract curve has been reached, it is not possible to make an amendment which is to the advantage of both parties. A movement along the curve would be to the advantage of one and to the disadvantage of the other. But there may be a great spread between the two ends of the contract curve. At one end all, or nearly all, the advantage goes to the one of the parties, nearly all to the other at the other end.

Although this construction was no more than a first step, it was already a considerable achievement. It throws a great deal of light on actual, practical, processes of bargaining—more, I think, than is thrown by Games Theory, which (perhaps because of its dependence on abstruse mathematical theorems which were quite outside Edgeworth's reach) has in latter days acquired such prestige. The particular application which Edgeworth had most in mind was to bargaining between a trade union and an employers' association;

167

and that is a field where it still has its uses. But one now wants to go on to still more important applications, to diplomatic bargaining between states, of which that now proceeding about armaments is a major example. In any of these cases one can see how a bargainer will often refuse a first step towards an agreement, corresponding to P_1 on the diagram I have been using, because he fears that it will set him on course towards a final contract, which, though it 'lies upon the contract curve' will be very unfavourable to him. It is the clash between absolute gain and relative gain which makes bargaining so difficult.

But now for competition. Proceed, at the next step, to introduce a second buyer and second seller, the two pairs being in contact. (All trades are still simple exchanges of good A for good B.) As Edgeworth very rightly shows, this need not by itself make much difference. What it does is to ensure that there can be no final settlement unless the same price is being charged throughout; the rate of exchange at which each pair is trading must be the same. For if it were not so, there would be a tendency to cross over—the less advantaged buyer changing to the seller from whom he could get better terms. But this does not imply that a very one-sided outcome, very favourable to the buyers (or to the sellers) is ruled out. For if separate bargainings had resulted in very similar settlements, then (whatever they were) competition so far would not upset them.

What makes the difference is when one seller can contract with more than one buyer (or vice versa). It is easiest to see this if one takes the case of employment of labour, which was Edgeworth's own example. Say that there are just two (possible) masters and two (possible) servants; I will venture to use those old terms which in this case are not inappropriate. Neither master minds which servant works for him, and neither servant minds which master he works for. Each servant will prefer to work for the master who offers better wages, and each master will prefer to employ the servant who will come for less. So if each master is to keep his servant, each must pay the same wage. But if the wage that was thus established was very low, it might be the case that a master would like to have two servants; but if he got both of them to work for him, the other master would get left out. So one can see him bidding up the wage, in order to keep his one servant for himself. Thus the extremely low wage, which at first sight seemed consistent with a final settlement, is not in fact consistent. The original set of practicable bargains, along the contract curve, is thus reduced in length. Though this does not make as good sense in the case of labour contracts (as Edgeworth noted) there should in principle be a similar closing-in at the other end.

The jump from employing one servant to employing two (as in this simple case) is *relatively* large; so the extent of closing-in, in this illustration, does not look considerable. But when the number of traders, on each side, is increased, the scope for re-arrangements, which will cause some party, on one side or the other, to get left out, becomes larger. It should not take a very large number to make the closing-in essentially complete. A market in which the closing in is complete, so that just one point on the contract curve is left, is what economists, ever since, have regarded as a perfect, or perfectly competitive, market.

I am not suggesting that Edgeworth invented the concept of a perfect market; it was there, in some of the works that he had read, in Cournot and Walras, at least. But by approaching it in the way that he did, he showed that the equilibrium of a perfectly competitive market would be such as could be represented by a point on his contract curve (suitably generalised). That is to say, there is no other set of bargains, which could be substituted for the equilibrium set, and which would not be worse than it is for some party, or parties. There may be other sets of bargains which would pass this test; but the equilibrium set of bargains is one that does pass it.

We are nowadays accustomed to express this proposition by saying that the equilibrium of perfect competition is a Pareto optimum; using that term as a tribute to the use that Pareto made of it. Still, Pareto got it from Edgeworth; there is no doubt of that.

A general proof of this Edgeworth-Pareto theorem, which will satisfy professional mathematicians, is quite difficult; but it is sufficient for most economic purposes just to note that the conditions for the establishment of a perfectly competitive equilibrium, and the conditions for a Pareto optimum, are the same. That Edgeworth clearly saw. So on this track, which has been followed by so many later economists, he did take the first step; and it is a defensible view that it was that first step which chiefly mattered.

That is as far as Edgeworth got, on the positive side, in *MP*; to what he said on the other (welfare) side I shall be coming in a moment. But before I come to that, I should like to say that he seems to me to have missed, at this point, an opportunity. He had given a rather full analysis of simple exchange, of quantities of two commodities (which I called A and B); he might have gone on to consider multiple exchange, in which more than two commodities come into question. He was already acquainted, when he wrote *MP*, with the work of Walras. Walras had gone on to study multiple exchange; but he had done so no more than set out equilibrium conditions. He could not explain the working of his market save by the introduction of his 'auctioneer', the device that Edgeworth rejected. A study of multiple exchange, on Edgeworth lines, would indeed have been more difficult. But if no more than the first steps towards it had been taken, things would have happened.

There can be no simple exchange (such as Edgeworth had been considering) between two parties unless each of them has things the other wants. But suppose that I have things I want to sell, and you have things you want to sell, but I do not want your goods, and you do not want mine.

But then suppose I can find another party, who will take my goods, though all he can offer in exchange is something I do not want. But these goods, which are not wanted by me, are wanted by you. Then I can get what I want, in exchange for what I have to sell, in two steps. (There may of course be more than two steps that are needed.) No final equilibrium, of Edgeworth type, can be achieved unless all such opportunities for indirect trade have been taken.

It will be noticed that it is essential, for such indirect trade to be possible, that there should be people who are willing to take in exchange, for the goods they have to sell, things which they do not themselves want, but are willing to take because they think it to be possible to hand them on to other people. People who take part in this sort of trade may appropriately be described as merchants. I don't think that Edgeworth could have constructed a model of multiple exchange, including indirect exchange, without introducing merchants. He would then have found that these merchants, each of them actual traders, seeking to make a profit, would have taken on most of the functions of Walras' 'auctioneer'.

It seems to me that it would have made a great deal of difference to the development of economic theory, in the years which followed, if Edgeworth had explored the route which I have just been trying to sketch out. For what that route leads to, very soon, is the introduction of *money*. Edgeworth himself never took much interest in monetary theory. Only in quite recent times has the power of an Edgeworthian approach to monetary theory begun to be realised.

So far, then, what Edgeworth had said had been very forward-

Francis Ysidro Edgeworth

looking; he has laid foundations for much of the work that economic theorists have been doing since his time. Of the final section of *MP* (on what he calls 'utilitarian calculus') that cannot be said. To understand it, one must remember that Edgeworth is a Utilitarian, in the strict sense that comes down from Bentham; the 'utility' or 'pleasure' that each individual is seeking to maximise is a quantity, and the aim of policy should be to maximise the sum of those quantities, all added together. Now if individuals are similar, and there is a general rule that marginal utility diminishes with wealth, it follows mathematically that this sum of utilities will be maximised if wealth is divided equally. Edgeworth clearly saw that (he was not the first to have seen it), but it is a conclusion that he was most unwilling to accept:

Consider Equality, the right of equals to equal advantages and burdens, that large section of distributive justice, that deep principle which continually upheaves the crust of convention.

> . . .πολλάων πολίων κατέλυσε κάρηνα
> ἠδ' ἔτι καὶ λύσει. του γὰρ κράτος ἐστι μέγιστον.

All this mighty moral force is deducible from the practicable principle of exact Utilitarianism combined with the simple laws of sentience (*a* and ß).

When one looks up this *a* and ß one finds that they are just the now familiar 'laws' of diminishing marginal utility and increasing marginal disutility).

I have inflicted on you the Homeric quotation, in the original Greek, pronounced as I was taught at school to pronounce it, and I suppose Edgeworth also; but I will venture to translate it, as it is essential to the force of the passage. It comes out, rather literally, as

Many are the states it has destroyed, and it will go on destroying. For its power is very great.

I am pretty sure that that is what Edgeworth meant.

Now if one wished to avoid that conclusion, while keeping to the strict Utilitarianism so dear to Edgeworth, the only way was to insist on inequality, inequality between persons, in ability to get 'pleasure' or to bear 'pain'. Perhaps what I said in the beginning about his forebears will help to explain why he took this line so strongly. Of course he was helped by the Darwinism, then so fashionable.

171

Sir John Hicks

Capacity for pleasure is a property of evolution, an essential attribute of civilisation. The grace of life, the charm of courtesy and courage, which once at least distinguished rank, not unreasonably received the means to enjoy and to transmit. To lower classes was assigned the work of which they seemed most capable; the work of the higher classes being different in kind was not to be equated in severity. If we suppose that capacity for pleasure is an attribute of skill and talent; if we consider that production is an unsymmetrical function of manual and scientific labour; we may see a reason deeper than Economics may afford [*he means, of course, his own positive economics*] for the larger pay, though often more agreeable work, of the aristocracy of skill and talent. The aristocracy of sex is similarly grounded upon the supposed superior capacity of the man for happiness, for the ἐνέϱγειαι of action and contemplation; upon the sentiment

'Woman is the lesser man, and her passions unto mine
Are as moonlight unto sunlight and as water unto wine'.

You will notice the 'supposes' with which these passages are studded; he does not commit himself to this Tennysonian outlook, but still leaves the impression that he is inclined to share it.

I do not know that there is any other economist who has gone so far in the direction of Inegalitarianism as Edgeworth in these passages appears to do. Even Pareto, who (as we have seen) was in many ways a follower of Edgeworth, and who undoubtedly shared Edgeworth's feelings on these matters, felt himself obliged to look for another way out. For him, it was the *strict* utilitarianism of Edgeworth that had caused the trouble. One can keep all that one needs of Jevonian (or Edgeworthian) utilitarianism if it is applied to individual choices only. Utility is just an index of preference, and there is no reason why the index that is used by one chooser, and that used by another, should be capable of being added up. So after Pareto (and after the work that was done by Robbins and others in publicising what had already been done by Pareto) economists need not feel themselves bound to be egalitarian, or anti-egalitarian. These are moral questions, on which not even the welfare economist need feel called on to pronounce.

But to go back to Edgeworth. There is a later work of his, on the *Theory of taxation*, in which he appears to take a very different line from that which he had taken in *MP*. This was written in 1897, sixteen years later. He there comes out, very strongly, in favour of what he calls the principle of 'minimum aggregate sacrifice', as opposed to that of 'equal sacrifice' which been championed by some of his contemporaries. As applied to taxation, his principle clearly tends in the direction of steeper progressiveness than the alternative. For now he has little to say about those differences in 'capacity for pleasure' of which in the earlier work he had made so much. It is evident, from the correspondence of Pareto, that Pareto (who had held firm to his inegalitarianism) thought that Edgeworth had been swayed by the influence of Marshall—that he had sold out to the Cambridge 'Left'.

But Edgeworth did not say that he had changed his mind, so perhaps he thought he had not done so. We must remember the date of the later paper. Progressive taxation was then a novelty. Even the Lloyd George budget of 1909 was still far ahead. No more than a very mild degree of progression was then in question. The total burden of taxation was still very low, in comparison with what it has since become, nearly everywhere. He could well have maintained that for the distribution of that burden, a government could not be expected to pay much attention to the (rather intangible) differences in capacity, of which he had made so much in *MP*. As long as progression remained as moderate, or nearly as moderate, as it was in the nineties, it did not threaten the destruction of which in *MP* he had been afraid.

There is that; but it may well be that there was something else. There is a very large part of Edgeworth's work of which in this paper I have said nothing. I did not feel myself called upon to discuss it, and I fear that I should have been quite incompetent to do so. His work on probability, on the foundations of statistical theory, is voluminous; it has never been brought together. There is a summary of it, by Bowley; but I am not sure, from the small sample I have made of the original writings, that Bowley represents him at all fully. To do justice to his work in this field would require a major effort of research, which I have been quite unable to undertake. It is not at all certain that it would be rewarding, for there is no question that Edgeworth's work in this field (as indeed in much of his economics) is peculiar. The line he worked out is treated with respect by some modern stochasticists; but it has not been generally followed. But that he has so strong an interest in this direction is one of the things that needs to be borne in mind.

There is a paper on 'The application of probability to economics' to be found in his collected papers, but I do not find it to be of much help. It is however to be noticed that (there at least) he endorses the classical *equally likely* principle—'the assumption that any probability-constant of which we know nothing is as likely to have one value as another'—the formulation he quotes himself. We know from other writings of his that he had some doubts about that principle (as others have done); but he was clearly willing, on occasion, to use it himself. I wonder whether it is not in some such way that he would have defended his later view on optimum taxation—against his earlier self, supposed to have risen up as critic. But that is only a guess.

It is indeed not only his work on statistical theory which in this paper I have largely overlooked. He did work on other parts of economics, on monopoly and on international trade, to take leading examples. It is chiefly my own taste which has led me to concentrate on *MP*, that admittedly early book. I do feel, myself, that I would rather lose those later papers than lose *Mathematical psychics*.